A BETTER DIRECTION

Researched and written by Kenneth Rea

A national enquiry into the training of directors for theatre, film and television

Kenneth Rea began as a professional actor and director in New Zealand. Although there was no training for directors, he learnt much from the late Tony Richardson, artistic director of the Mercury Theatre, Auckland, and former director of the Belgrade Theatre, Coventry. At the age of 23 he formed his own company, The Living Theatre Troupe.

In 1976 he came to Britain where he has continued to direct. In addition to his regular teaching at the Guildhall School of Music and Drama, he has conducted workshops for a number of theatres, including the Royal Shakespeare Company, as well as teaching abroad, in China, Canada, Indonesia and Singapore.

He also works as a theatre critic for *The Guardian* and contributes regularly to BBC's *Meridian* and *Kaleidoscope*. His children's play *The Frankenstein Case* was performed in New Zealand last year.

Published by Calouste Gulbenkian Foundation, London, 1989

Further copies are available from the
Calouste Gulbenkian Foundation, UK Branch
98 Portland Place
London W1N 4ET

© 1989 Calouste Gulbenkian Foundation
ISBN 0 903319 49 7
Designed by The Upper Room

*"How much better
we might have been
had we been
properly trained."*

Peter Hall

CONTENTS

I

II

III

IV

V

VI

VII

VIII

IX

X

7

In writing this report I have given considerable space to the profile of the director in order to provide a clear context for the training needs. Inevitably this opens up the important discussion of how directors work, which really needs fuller treatment outside this Enquiry.

Throughout the report I have used direct quotations where these would express a view more vividly and concisely than reported speech or a summary. Some of the quotes are taken from written submission, but most are from transcripts of interviews and seminars: only minor grammatical adjustments have been made so that the two modes blend satisfactorily. For the sake of compression, a great deal had to be omitted and I apologize to those people who made similar observations but have not been quoted.

I would like to thank the many hundreds of people who gave evidence to the Enquiry for the frankness and candour with which they expressed their views. This has helped greatly to strengthen the overall tone of the report and identify the key issues.

I am also deeply indebted to the tireless enthusiasm of the Working Party. Their commitment to the Enquiry has been inestimable. Without their help in collecting the evidence and their advice in nursing the report through its various drafts, the end result would never have been so thorough. Particular thanks are due to our chairman, Edward Braun, for his meticulous attention to the manuscript and to Iain Reid, Assistant Director, Arts, at the UK Branch of the Gulbenkian Foundation - he was the inspiration and the guiding force behind the Enquiry.

Among the many individuals who have assisted the Enquiry, I am particularly grateful to John Ainslie of British Actors' Equity, Suzan Dormer of the Directors Guild of Great Britain, Olwen Wymark of the Writers' Guild of Great Britain and Michael Baker, Drama Director of the Welsh Arts Council.

My special thanks also to Millicent Bowerman and Lynne Cope for their editorial help, and to Nicola Howe who was the secretarial assistant to the Enquiry. Finally, I thank my wife for putting up with it all.

Kenneth Rea

July, 1989

Foreword

For the past twenty years or more gatherings of theatre practi.ioners, teachers and administrators have regularly debated the role of the director and the need for training. Notwithstanding the weary claims (usually from ill-used actors) that directing is a mere distemper that will shortly have run its troublesome course, a broad consensus has emerged around the view that the director is both necessary and needs to be trained. Beyond that, as the findings of this Enquiry show, views diverge.

Film and television present a less confused picture: under-resourced as training is in most institutions, it tends to pursue shared objectives dictated by the specific requirements of the production process. Nowadays, few would question the definition of the director offered by *The Oxford Companion to Film:* "the principal creative artist involved in the making of any film; the artistic supervisor of the work performed by the other artists and technicians, and of the form and content of the film itself."

Significantly, Bradby and Williams in their recent *Directors' Theatre* employ much more general terms to characterize the advance of the stage director: "In the last hundred years...the director has progressed from the role of simple stage manager to the position of central power in the theatre enterprise." 'Power' and 'theatre enterprise': the words accurately reflect the importance of many directors today and the formidable scope of their responsibilities. Yet, compared with most other major theatre cultures, Britain offers little or no structured training for this most crucial of functions, and dwindling resources to fund the little that does exist.

There is a danger that the recent growth of 'actors' theatre', admirable as it may be, will tend to undermine the case for the director and perhaps serve to widen the gulf that undoubtedly separates many actors and directors. The evidence of this Enquiry should counter any such tendency: the response from right across the profession, in strength of numbers and in depth of concern, argues powerfully for a better-equipped, better-informed and better-resourced directorial culture to the greater benefit, not only of the director, but of the playwright, the performer, the designer, the stage-manager, the music-director, the administrator - and the spectator alike. It is the job of an enquiry to articulate concern and to suggest means of responding to it. But unless it leads to the release of new money to achieve its objectives, it will become just one more work of reference on library shelves. Let that not be the fate of *A Better Direction.*

Edward Braun

July, 1989

Background to the Enquiry

In October 1986 the Calouste Gulbenkian Foundation funded a three-day symposium on directors' training, organized by the Directors Guild of Great Britain. One of the recommendations of this symposium was that an enquiry was needed. The Directors' Training Enquiry (whose evidence, conclusions and recommendations are laid out in this report) was set up by the Calouste Gulbenkian Foundation in the autumn of 1987 following approaches from various sectors of the theatre profession who were concerned about standards of directing and about the widespread lack of knowledge amongst directors of both the technical and creative processes. Directors themselves were unhappy at the lack of opportunities for training.

The Directors' Training Enquiry was set up under the chairmanship of Professor Edward Braun, Head of Drama at the University of Bristol and Chairman of the Bristol Old Vic Theatre. The Working Party met regularly between October 1987 and April 1989 to discuss the objectives and strategy of the Enquiry and to evaluate its findings. The Working Party comprised:

Mike Alfreds (director)

Paul Bassett (general manager, Citizens Theatre)

Yvonne Brewster (director)

John Glenister (television director)

Sheila Kelley (actor) until June 1988

Jane Lapotaire (actor)

Mike Leigh (director) until June 1988

Adrian Noble (director)

Chrissie Poulter (deputy director, Yorkshire Arts)

Janet Suzman (actor)

Harriet Walter (actor)

This was not intended as a representative panel; wide representation of views was sought through the range of the Enquiry.

Ian Brown (Director of Drama, Arts Council of Great Britain) was the consultant.

Kenneth Rea (writer and drama tutor) was the researcher and author.

1. Aims

Our brief was to investigate the existing provision for director training, both in Britain and abroad, in theatre (including opera), film, television and radio. We were also to find out how directors have developed their skills, and to determine the range of skills that a director requires to work effectively in any given medium at any level. If our researches pointed to conclusions which needed solutions, we were invited to make recommendations.

2. Working method

The Enquiry was launched in November 1987 with a press release inviting contributions from individuals and organizations. Shortly afterwards a questionnaire was sent to more than 2,000 directors in theatre, opera, film, television and radio: the 640 replies were computer-analysed by Dr Gordon Reece of Bristol University. This analysis has provided by far the most comprehensive information yet assembled on directors and their views on director training.

In the course of the Enquiry members of the Working Party visited a broad selection of courses and schemes offering director training, 20 in all. Written information was obtained from other courses in this country and abroad.

In response to suggestions from umbrella organizations and individuals, letters were sent inviting submissions from a further 130 directors and from 81 other members of the profession including actors, writers, designers, choreographers and technicians. Nearly half of these people submitted evidence.

Regional meetings were set up in Bristol, Cardiff, Glasgow, Manchester, Leeds and London. Each of these comprised a session with people from across the profession and a session with directors only. A separate meeting of opera personnel was held in London and a meeting of playwrights at the Writers' Guild of Great Britain. Finally, members of the Working Party interviewed selected directors, actors and other specialists. In all, evidence was taken from more than 1,000 people.

3. Research

Most of our research concerned director training in theatre, film and television: there was an emphasis on theatre because in this area there is such poor provision. Our research revealed a strong feeling in favour of a structured training for directors to include:
a) basic technical instruction,
b) the study of dramatic literature and culture and
c) an element of attachment that would allow some exposure to the profession.

In putting forward our solutions and recommendations it should be noted that we have considered opinions and advice from a wide variety of people in all branches of drama, live and recorded. Our conclusions therefore are based on what the profession thinks, not only directors of all kinds but the people who work with them. The Equity paper (see Appendix A) was a valuable starting point and a great help in our discussions. It offers one of several solutions.

The provisions for director training in film and television were found to be more or less adequate, with minor additions and modifications which will be described.

In the time available we have not been able to identify the needs in opera, dance and radio in the same detail with which we have examined the other media. Our research indicates that training in radio is adequate, but in opera it is meagre, taking advantage of the fact that most directors tend to have extensive prior experience in theatre. Dance needs a closer examination of the way that choreographers go about staging their work and communicating their ideas. This is perhaps the subject for another more specialized study.

Although we were not able to examine fully the question of disabilities in director training, our research revealed no discrimination in this area. Director training for the amateur sector has not been covered because our brief was to confine ourselves to training for the profession. We were aware that there are director training courses at an amateur level, but again, this is a subject for a separate study.

PART ONE

THE DIRECTOR

Part 1 The director

Chapter I

WHAT IS A DIRECTOR?

I

1. Historical Background to Directing

Directing, as we think of it today, is a recent phenomenon in the history of the theatre. Whilst it is safe to assume that someone has always been responsible for rehearsing any play on the stage, it was not until the nineteenth century that the director as such emerged.

As the urge for ever more extravagant spectacle seized the theatre, actor-managers such as Charles Kean and Samuel Phelps achieved remarkable displays of scenic art which demanded lengthy rehearsal and close attention to costume and settings. However, there was little concern with the interpretation of the play-text and its coherent expression through the full range of the theatre's means of expression: this dimension was introduced to theatre production by the Duke of Saxe-Meiningen and his stage director, Ludwig Chronegk, whose provincial company first appeared in Berlin in 1874. By demanding adequate rehearsal time and by paying attention to the dynamic possibilities of crowd scenes, they were able to weld the production into a disciplined, organic whole. The impact made by the Meiningen company on European theatre was enormous.

In France during the late 1880s André Antoine pursued Zola's principles of naturalism on stage, both in acting and staging, and his example was soon taken up by Stanislavsky in Russia. By this time the director as an interpretive artist was becoming an indispensable figure in the modern theatre.

By the turn of the century directors were finding differing ways of interpreting the text or, as it often turned out, freely expressing their own vision. In consequence the importance of the actor's contribution was diminishing in favour of the mise-en-scène. At its most extreme this trend led to the director assuming dictatorial power over the actors and virtually every aspect of the production. ''Until discipline is understood in a theatre to be willing and reliant obedience to the director...no supreme achievement can be accomplished,'' wrote Edward Gordon Craig in 1905.

The influence of Craig, Meyerhold, Rheinhardt and others set the predominant tone for directing in the twentieth century. Over the past 80 years the director has often been as strong an influence on the course of theatre as the playwright. However, this tendency has been more pronounced in the rest of Europe than it has in Britain. The bold concepts that typify the productions of Peter Stein, Giorgio Strehler, Patrice Chereau, Tadeusz Kantor or Yuri Lyubimov are admired but rarely emulated in Britain where so-called 'directors' theatre' is less fashionable.

The development of directing in Britain has tended to follow a middle way where close collaboration with the actors and deep respect for the text are valued. It was only relatively recently that the interpretive potential of the director's role was realized. As Peggy Ashcroft recalled, ''When I went into the theatre, I couldn't find a director. In those days one didn't sit down and read the play and discuss it. You were placed - roughly. And you sank or swam.''

William Poel, Harley Granville-Barker and later, John Gielgud, had all done exemplary work in their Shakespearean productions, but the model of what the director could be was set by Tyrone Guthrie, the most dominant influence on British directing in the mid-twentieth century.

Another strand of directing in Britain originated in Paris in the 1920s with Jacques Copeau, being brought to this country in the 1930s by one of Copeau's pupils, Michel Saint-Denis. Through his work at the London Theatre Studio and later at the Old Vic Theatre School, Saint-Denis had a profound effect on the training of actors and directors.

In the past two decades the range of theatre in Britain has widened to include theatre-in-education, community theatre, mime theatre, physical theatre, circus theatre, and a variety of experimental and performance-art styles. The director's role in these genres varies considerably. There will not always be a text to interpret; often the company will function as a collective with the director having a very low profile. A key source of this collective approach was the work of Joan Littlewood, particularly after 1953 when with Gerry Raffles she began to work at the Theatre Workshop, Stratford East. No one more thoroughly assimilated the ideas of Brecht than Joan Littlewood, and her influence on the modern British stage is incalculable. Perhaps more than any director she exemplifies the perfect fusion of ensemble work and spontaneity.

Theatre evolved through the play, thus it required a writer; the lasting trends and movements in theatre are most clearly signified by playwrights rather than directors.

The development of directing in film and television has taken a different course. Film began with a moving image, thus it required a director and a performer. The story was told entirely in pictures: the silent era. When sound was introduced and words were needed, writers were hired to write, essentially to the order of powerful producers and directors. That is still true, though changing - not so much through writers achieving any real autonomous power as through directors recognizing and sharing the creative responsibility with writers, and through writers becoming their own directors.

This development is generally true for British and North American film culture. In Europe and further East the emphasis is on the auteur director - the complete cinematic artist, conceiving, writing and directing a film to make a personal observation or statement. What many of these various film directors have in common is an absence of any formal training, chiefly because there was little opportunity for it until relatively recently. They learnt by working in some other branch of film-making, observing and absorbing from their peers. The director in the cinema is a powerful presence and the development of cinema can be traced through directorial styles.

Television was preceded by radio, in particular, BBC radio. It was not influenced at all by film in any cinematic sense. The traditions of radio broadcasting were made visible, but not visual. It was at first an illustrated verbal medium of talking heads. The genesis of the TV director was from a naïve beginning, hampered by heavy, cumbersome and unreliable equipment and the constraints of broadcasting live. The drama work was the studio presentation of stage plays with the cameras observing the action as if from three or four different seats in the stalls. The director's task was chiefly to keep it all going for 90 minutes or more - an achievement in itself. Such a production would have required the ability of a competent theatre director.

The influences that changed the skills and status of the TV director include early visionary directors like Rudolph Cartier, Christian Simpson, Ian Atkins and Dennis Vance, who began to experiment with form and content; the coming of ITV in 1955 and with it the enormous influence of the Canadian school led by Sydney Newman and manifested in Armchair Theatre; and the pioneering work in America of directors like Delbert Mann and Sidney Lumet working with writers like Paddy Chayefsky and Reginald Rose, to produce such work as *Bachelor Party, Marty* and *Twelve Angry Men*. This probably marked the beginning of the TV director as a major contributor to the artistic whole of a TV drama - and of writing for TV as a specific talent. Other processes that produced far-reaching changes were the advent of recorded television, editing, film inserts, light-weight equipment and greater mobility. The craft of the director was continually having to be re-learnt.

British TV reached a peak of directing skills in the 1960s from which most current techniques and styles derive. A few landmark productions would include the *Monitor* films, the *Tonight* film reports, *That Was The Week That Was, The Wednesday Play* and the socially committed drama/documentaries, as well as many memorable literary and historical dramatisations. Now, with the extensive use of all-film and single-camera video shooting, the TV director has begun, after some 40 years, to work like a film director and most of the required disciplines in TV are identical to those in cinema. In fact the director will often work in both fields, which was unthinkable some 20 years ago.

Beyond the network of television programmes a fairly recent development has been the rapid growth of a whole new industry demanding fresh disciplines and sophisticated visual techniques - the advertising commercial and the pop-music promotional film and video. Even so, television will probably still require a multi-camera 'live' presentational skill in order to maintain studio-based programmes such as soap-operas, panel games, quiz and chat shows, magazine and news programmes. The training for these skills cannot be ignored.

2. The Director's Function Today

In considering the training of the director we had to be clear on the question: training for what? It is therefore appropriate to begin with an understanding of the function of the director.

It can be appreciated that the director today serves a useful purpose in the staging of drama, both live and recorded. Almost invariably attempts to supplant the director have ended with someone else in the group taking on that function. Ironically, when actors have turned to directing they have often imposed themselves more strongly than some of the directors they reacted against.

a. Definition

When we asked people from across the profession what they thought a director was (and this embraced both live and recorded media) the responses indicated that the role was seen primarily as interpretive rather than creative, although it was recognized that the job requires a creative temperament. At the same time there is a strong feeling that the director is there to draw out the best from the creative efforts of the rest of the team. The job therefore involves setting up the conditions in which people can do their best work.

Some of the most common definitions were: 'an enabler,' 'a catalyst,' 'a co-ordinator,' 'the trustee of the writer,' 'an organizer,' 'a collaborator - the first among equals,' 'a chairman of the committee,' 'the one who stands outside,' 'a team leader,' ' a person who creates an atmosphere in which other people can create.'

This contrasts with attitudes abroad where the director is widely regarded - and accepted - as more of a dictator. As Stuart Burge observed, the emphasis in Germany at the moment is not on writing, it is on presentation; in this country it happens that the emphasis is more on text.

b. Function

The function of the director will vary according to the medium and genre. The demands on a director of experimental and devised work, for example, are quite different from the demands on someone who is staging a classical play, while a film makes other demands. But the necessary qualities common to all directors are the ability to make the play or film communicate and to recognize the collaborative nature of the job. The director's function might therefore be seen as serving the audience, the playwright and the actors equally.

Almost all the people we heard from stressed the vital need for a director to have contact with the whole team involved in the production - actors and technical staff alike. We heard complaints about young directors on attachment, just out of university, often lacking a sense of respect for stage managers and actors. Should training, at least in part, be linked with the working profession?

The ability to generate energy was considered a quality common to great directors and indeed Guthrie has written, "The all-important thing for a director is not to let rehearsals be a bore." Of course this alone does not guarantee a great production and care needs to be taken that energy does not become a pointless end in itself.

It is significant that many of those thought to be the finest directors appear to work in a very flexible and open way. However, several of them admitted that they began their careers by meticulously mapping out every move in advance, only to abandon this approach once they became aware of how much the actors had to contribute. Those regarded as inferior directors, on the other hand, tend to remain more rigid and less willing to involve the actors. Even so, views differed on the degree to which a director should be prepared to improvise as opposed to sticking to a rigid plan in rehearsals. An ideal is to go into rehearsals prepared but totally open to what the team will contribute. As Declan Donnellan explained, "Each time I do a show, I don't feel I bring any experience from a previous show to it. At the start of the rehearsal period I walk into that room with my heart in the pit of my stomach thinking I'm bringing nothing into this room with me. Yet I may know the script by heart."

For Clive Barker, who spent many years working as an actor with Joan Littlewood, the mark of a good director is how late he/she will leave it to structure the actors' performance through direction. "Littlewood would leave it until three days before opening. On several occasions we didn't manage a dress rehearsal. Her ability to leave the moment that late relied on the quality she has concealed and which she has never been given credit for - a formidable technique. She could structure and re-structure scenes and compose stage pictures and images with amazing speed and sureness."

Balancing the director's contribution against those of the actors calls for sensitive judgement. There was much criticism of the tendency amongst directors to impose their ideas on a production simply to achieve an effect or make their mark upon it. But many directors defended the need for a strong, well thought-out line in rehearsals. As Trevor Nunn put it, "It is no good being the director of something and being so utterly diffident that you are just a chairman or a conduit for other people's thoughts. If that's the way, it's false pretences, it's a complete waste of time."

It is generally recognized that directors, particularly in the early stages of their career, are ambitious and may feel under a certain pressure to make an impact on the profession. Even the best of today's senior directors suffered from this in their early years. The danger is that under this pressure the true functions of the director can easily be lost or distorted. What is difficult for young directors to appreciate is that the finest direction often draws the least attention to itself. Could proper training encourage a more productive attitude?

"I am finding more and more what I call the 'director as artiste' principle," said Terry Hands. "It's not an involvement with bringing the actors out, but expressing themselves. That used not to be the case - in this country.''

Many directors emphasized that it is always unproductive to treat actors like puppets, however some underlined the manipulative aspects of the job. While Alan Strachan thought direction was essentially a collaborative rather than a dictatorial process, he saw the director's function as being ''to guide, by whatever means possible or necessary - including cajoling, guile, persuasion or even, on occasion, considerable pressure (some would even add bullying) - a cast towards this final process.''

The view was also defended that sometimes a play and a cast need to be subjected to a strong individual conception where the director acts more as auteur. ''We all do that sometimes, and often get our best reviews when we do,'' admitted Ronan Patterson. ''It is not always honest, but it is sometimes necessary. At other times we might have a good script and a good cast who really just need to be allowed to get on with it, with the occasional word of encouragement, or selection between options.''

i. Film

In film the co-ordinating aspect of the work is one of the most vital functions and the director must have a good understanding of other people's jobs in the production team in order to get the best out of them. The ability to evolve a script in collaboration with the writer is also essential. In every area the director has enormous power. Many film directors have also taken on the role of auteur creating their own script, though as already noted, this is a trend more common in European cinema than in Britain.

The function of the film director is partly confused by the contrasting intentions different directors will have. One director may set out to create a surrealistic piece in which the actors are little more than figures on the landscape, while another director may put strong acting performances above all else. According to Richard Attenborough, one of the problems is that critics and the media are often guilty of craving for the evidence of a directorial style. Consequently, ''an awful lot of directors, particularly relatively young directors who are beginning, believe that the imprint of their style is in fact a pre-requisite to their being noticed. I believe the antithesis. I believe the style is the correct style if it suits the particular subject matter and the form in which you decide to convey that subject. Camera pyrotechnics are not really of great interest to me. If I have a style, it is an unobtrusive style.''

Either way, it is a job in which there are enormous pressures. Because of the logistics of film-making and the expense involved, most of the creative decisions must be planned well in advance, allowing only a minimum of improvising when one actually gets behind the camera. The director must also be able to work with large numbers of people without wasting time.

Furthermore, film-making has evolved in such a way that when everyone is on the set the technical aspects tend to take priority over the actors' needs. Jack Gold pointed out that, compared with other departments, the director working with the actors has the least time of all: ''A take may last two minutes for a scene, and if you have three or four, that's eight minutes, say. And with a bit of rehearsal, allow an hour. So out of the day, for a two or three minute scene you've had about an hour's work and everybody else has had four or five.''

ii. Television

The function of the television director can be seen as leading, guiding and inspiring a large team with very different skills to a common end. That goal may be a director's vision, a writer's vision or a collaborative effort, but there will always be a script as a starting point. In this sense it is similar to the film director working in cinema.

One important difference between the television and cinema director is that, generally speaking, the television director (and writer) still enjoy rather more creative freedom because the commercial pressure on their product is not as great. This, of course, could change if the worst fears about the deregulation of broadcasting are realized.

The contrast between working in film and television and working in the theatre is, according to Christopher Morahan, largely to do with the power that the director has over the final product. In film and television, he said, ''The director has the power to choose, to decide A or B or C. Whereas in the theatre, in a way, the actors' presence and your own immobility, sitting in the middle of the stalls, shaking like a leaf, means that when it comes to the first night you have no power at all. All you've done is pass on objectives and ways of achieving them. Then they're on their own. Whereas the film or television director has control of events, so that eventually what is completed is 'it'. It's finite. Whereas in theatre you don't complete 'it', because 'it' never exists.''

Chapter II

PROFILE OF THE DIRECTOR

II

We considered it important to find out where directors come from because many people we heard from talked about background as a means of explaining the way directors are, using terms like 'middle class' or 'graduate'. This information would enable us to determine whether certain groups of people have a more privileged start in the profession, whether there is evidence of discrimination or unequal opportunity and how great a role education or training plays in the director's career.

An examination of the kind of people who become directors reveals that the patterns are changing. While the older director tends to be Oxbridge, male and ex-public school, among the younger generation there is a higher presence of women directors, less Oxbridge dominance, but a greater degree of university education. Thus, eight out of ten directors under 30 are graduates, while only half of the directors over 50 graduated.

The questionnaire yielded many useful details on the backgrounds of the kind of people who direct. 640 returns were received and processed by Dr Gordon Reece of Bristol University (NB all figures are rounded up to the nearest percentage point). Dr Reece emphasized that the overall pattern of the statistics stabilized itself quite early on in the processing, so that the growing number of returns merely reinforced the earlier findings. This suggests that the figures we have are probably quite accurate for the whole sample of 2,300 who were invited to reply. It should also be noted that a return of just under a third is extremely high for a questionnaire of this kind.

For convenience, we asked directors to classify themselves as 'working mainly' in theatre (spoken drama on stage), opera, television, film or radio.

Percentage of respondents

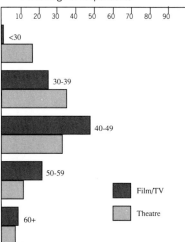

1. Theatre

A large majority of British theatre directors are white, male graduates of public school background who have had no formal training as directors. Taking all ages, 71% are male, 29% female.

a. Age and Experience

TABLE 1 - AGE

The profession seems to be dominated by mature directors, no doubt because people continue working as directors for a considerable time, accumulating experience. 64% of all theatre directors are in their 30s or 40s; 20% are over 50; only 15% of directors are under 30. This suggests that a significant proportion must have begun directing when they were over 30, which is an important factor to consider when examining training provisions.

Viewed another way, 45% of theatre directors have been doing the job for less than 10 years, 29% have been directing for between 10 and 20 years, 19% have been directing for 20 to 30 years and 7% have had more than 30 years' experience of directing.

b. Ethnic Background

TABLE 2 - ETHNIC ORIGIN

15% of directors were born outside Britain and only 3% gave their ethnic origin as being non-European. Clearly, this indicates very few black British directors working in this country.

c. Educational Background

The pattern of success is perhaps established very early on, in secondary education. 39% of theatre directors have come from independent schools, which is extremely high, considering that the overall national figure for independent school education is only 7% (1988). The figure was even lower a decade ago (5.7% in 1978) when many of today's younger directors were at school. Of the rest, 41% attended a grammar school and 22% attended a comprehensive. Adjustment is necessary here since grammar schools began to be phased out in the 1950s and comprehensive education did not become established until the early 1960s.

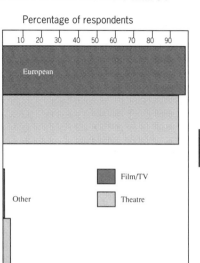

Percentage of respondents

TABLE 3 - EDUCATION (SECONDARY)

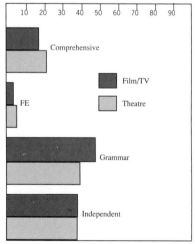

Percentage of respondents

University education is becoming an increasingly important factor in the backgrounds of theatre directors. Overall, 71% are graduates (this includes graduates from polytechnics, higher education colleges and other institutions). It should be remembered however that as late as 1963 only three universities (Bristol, Manchester and Hull) had drama departments, so most of the older directors who attended university were not studying drama. Today there are many more drama departments in universities and colleges and it is more likely that a student who wants to become a director will choose one of these in preference to Oxford or Cambridge, neither of which offers formal drama courses.

Percentage of respondents

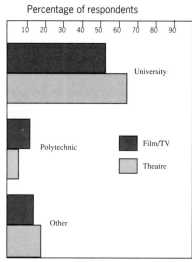

TABLE 4 - EDUCATION (TERTIARY)

An examination of the age range, taken over all categories, shows that while a high proportion of older directors have been to public school, fewer of them went to university. 50% of those over 60 are graduates, 54% in their 50s, 63% in their 40s, 74% in their 30s and 83% of the under 30s have graduated. This indicates that nearly all the younger generation of directors coming into the profession are graduates.

d. Drama Departments

Significantly only 4% of all working theatre directors have come out of university or polytechnic drama departments. This suggests that these departments have yet to make their full impact on the profession. At the same time it should be noted that most drama departments do not aim to provide vocational training.

e. Male/Female Ratios

Most university and higher education drama departments determine their male/female ratio of students in proportion to the ratio of applicants. But there is a discrepancy here: roughly twice as many women apply to study drama at universities as men, whilst in the theatre profession nearly three times more men than women find work as directors. As more students are encouraged to make their own opportunities - such as setting up their own companies - the proportion of women directors working in Britain is likely to increase over the next decade.

Percentage of respondents

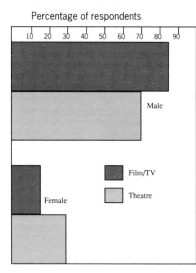

TABLE 5 - GENDER

This is reflected in the figures across all categories. While only 4% of all male directors are under 30, 20% of all female directors are under 30. Looked at in another way, of all those directors under 30, 43% are male and 57% are female. Compare this with directors in their 50s: 92% are male and 8% are female. But while the percentage of young women directors has risen, the figures also indicate that more women tend to leave the profession by the time they are 50.

f. Formal Training

As most of today's working theatre directors entered the profession before university drama courses became widely available, it is not surprising that the proportion without formal director training is relatively high: 64% across all age groups. Of those who did have director training, most were trained in a drama school (17%). Across all categories (theatre, film and TV) 55% of directors had no formal director training.

Percentage of respondents

TABLE 6 - % WHO HAVE RECEIVED FORMAL TRAINING

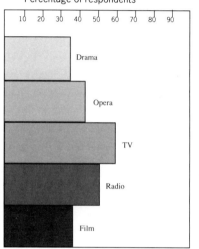

Against this 9% had come through one of the very few professional courses or schemes available.

54% of all working directors had no formal training whatsoever in any branch of the profession. When one compares the rigid standards now applied to actor training (or to the training of a musician) this figure is alarmingly high for a job that commands so much power and responsibility - given, of course, that one accepts training as necessary for a director.

g. Acting Experience

Many directors have made the transition from acting. It is interesting to note that 76% of all theatre directors have acted professionally at some time (taking into account the above paragraph, it must be assumed that many of them were not trained as actors). Others acted in the course of their training, and only 14% have had no experience of acting at all.

Percentage of respondents

TABLE 7 - % WHO HAVE ACTED PROFESSIONALLY

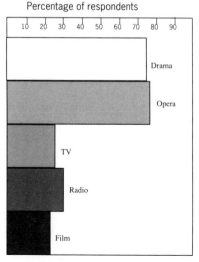

h. Type of Directing Experience

Individual initiative seems to be an important factor among theatre directors. 60% had at some point set up their own company.

In our questionnaire we asked directors to list the types of companies they had worked for professionally. This gives an accurate indication of where the work lies in British theatre.

Percentage of respondents

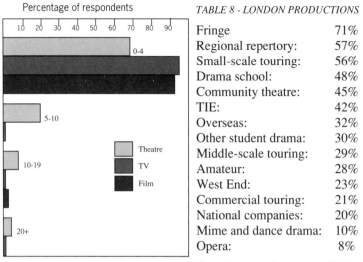

TABLE 8 - LONDON PRODUCTIONS

Fringe	71%
Regional repertory:	57%
Small-scale touring:	56%
Drama school:	48%
Community theatre:	45%
TIE:	42%
Overseas:	32%
Other student drama:	30%
Middle-scale touring:	29%
Amateur:	28%
West End:	23%
Commercial touring:	21%
National companies:	20%
Mime and dance drama:	10%
Opera:	8%

Over the past three years 70% of directors had between one and four theatre productions in London.

i. Amount of Work

As several directors commented, it is very difficult to earn a living in the theatre as a freelance director because it is necessary to do a great many productions to make sufficient money. Artistic directors and staff directors are in a better position here, though compared with the number of productions a director on the Continent might be expected to do in a year, the average

Percentage of respondents

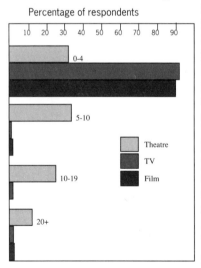

number in this country remains high. Of those who answered our questionnaire, 32% had done between one and four productions in the past three years, 33% had done between five and ten productions, 25% had done between ten and nineteen productions and 9% had done more than twenty productions. This means that at least 10% of directors have been doing seven or more productions a year: that is an average of one production every seven weeks. An established director on the Continent might expect at least six months rehearsal for a single production, if not a whole year.

TABLE 9 - TOTAL PRODUCTIONS

28

j. Earnings

Paid work for theatre directors is not usually continuous. For the financial year 1986-87 less than a third of directors had 39 or more paid weeks of work in the theatre. Another 30% had between one and 12 weeks paid work, and 20% had no paid work at all. Not surprisingly, just over half of theatre directors used their skills in some other form of work to support themselves: this was usually teaching, lecturing or leading workshops.

Clearly, not many people are making much money out of directing. More than half earned £5,000 per annum.

Gross earnings as a director for the financial year 1986-87 were as follows:

Under	£ 1,000	22%
£ 1,000 -	£ 5,000	29%
£ 5,000 -	£10,000	17%
£10,000 -	£15,000	12%
£15,000 -	£20,000	4%
£20,000 -	£30,000	3%
Over	£30,000	2%

(11% declined to answer this question)

2. Opera

Our sample of opera directors was much smaller than that of theatre directors, but there are far fewer job opportunities. Our figures also exclude opera directors who consider themselves mainly theatre directors. Even so, the picture is similar to that of the theatre though there is a stronger male presence and a more extreme educational pattern.

a. Male/Female Ratio

Taking all ages, 78% of opera directors are male; 22% female.

b. Age and Experience

Opera is dominated by older directors: over half of them are in their 40s; 11% are in their 50s; 22% are in their 30s; and only 11% are under 30.

The length of experience in directing is equally divided. A third have directed for less than 10 years, a third for between 10 and 20 years, and a third for between 20 and 30 years. No one has more than 30 years directing experience, which suggested that opera directors retire earlier than theatre directors.

c. Ethnic Origin

All the opera directors who answered our questionnaire were born in Britain of European origin. The survey indicates few, if any, black British opera directors.

d. Educational Background

Public school education accounts for 78% of opera directors (against the present national average of 7%); the rest went to a grammar school, and none to a comprehensive. 78% of opera directors were university graduates.

e. Formal Training

The proportion of opera directors who have had some sort of formal director training is higher than that of theatre directors. A third have been trained in a drama school and only just over a half had no director training at all.

Only 22% of opera directors have had no formal theatre training of any kind compared with 40% of theatre directors.

f. Experience of Acting

Most opera directors have had experience of acting. 78% have acted professionally; 22% have never acted at all.

g. Types of Directing Experience

In our questionnaire we also asked opera directors to list the types of theatre companies they had worked for professionally in addition to opera. (The high proportion of amateur involvement may account for amateur opera productions where the director was paid.)

Amateur:	78%	National companies:	33%
Overseas:	56%	Fringe:	22%
Drama school:	55%	Commercial touring:	22%
Small-scale touring:	44%	Middle-scale touring:	11%
Other student drama:	44%	Community theatre:	nil
Regional repertory:	33%	TIE:	nil
West End:	33%	Mime and dance drama:	nil

In the past three years 56% of directors have done between one and four productions in London.

h. Amount of Work

Employment conditions in opera seem to be slightly better than in theatre. 56% of opera directors had more than 39 paid weeks in the financial year 1986-87. This probably refers to staff directors with opera companies. Freelancers find it harder: 44% had between one and twelve paid weeks work, and 22% had no paid work at all for that year. 55% of opera directors used their skills in some other related work to supplement their income.

Of those who answered our questionnaire, a third had done between one and four productions in the past three years; 22% had done between five and ten productions; and a third had done more than twenty productions. This last figure, which implies an average of one production every seven weeks, may also be influenced by staff directors staging revivals with minimal rehearsal. It does imply a very high turnover of work for a third of opera directors.

i. Earnings

As in the case of theatre directors it seems that not very many people earn a lot from directing opera. A third earned less than £1,000. The absence of high earners (over £30,000) in our figures may indicate a lack of statistical information, or it may be found in the 11% who declined to answer this question.

Gross earnings as a director for the financial year 1986-87 were as follows:

Under £ 1,000	33%
£ 1,000 - £ 5,000	nil
£ 5,000 - £10,000	11%
£10,000 - £15,000	22%
£15,000 - £20,000	22%
£20,000 - £30,000	nil
Over £30,000	nil

(11% declined to answer this question)

3. Television

British television directors on the whole conform to the pattern of white, male graduates, though there is a higher incidence of directors who have been trained. No doubt this is because considerable technical knowledge is required to direct a television play, without which entry into the profession would be difficult. It also reflects the fact that both the BBC and Independent Television companies have been running their own training courses for some time.

Although our figures refer to television directors who direct, or have directed, drama, it should be remembered that many of these people will also have worked on documentary, current affairs, light entertainment and other areas outside drama.

a. Male/Female Ratio

Television directing is overwhelmingly weighted in favour of men. Taking all ages, 83% are male; 17% female.

b. Age and Experience

It is a profession in which young people are rare. Only 4 television directors in every 100 are under 30. The largest group, 46%, are in their 40s; 24% are in their 30s; 23% are in their 50s; and 7% are over 60. There is a predominance of more experienced directors. While 29% of them have been directing for less than 10 years; 36% have between 10 and 20 years' directing experience; and 35% have been directing for more than 20 years.

c. Ethnic Origin

13% were born outside Britain and only 1% gave their ethnic origin as being non-European. Thus, there seem to be hardly any black British directors working in British television.

d. Educational Background

Public school education once again features highly: 41% of television directors have been to an independent school. Just under half attended grammar school and 15% attended a comprehensive. Higher education is the norm. 67% of television directors are graduates; 12% went to a polytechnic.

e. Formal Training

The evidence of formal director training is higher than for theatre directors, although 40% of television directors without any director training still seems quite high. Of those who were trained, 4% have been to a drama school; 18% have been to a film and television school; 1% have been to a university or polytechnic drama department; and 27% have been on a professional course, which emphasizes that film and television have a much more developed in-service provision. A further 16% have been on shorter workshops and in-house training schemes.

These figures indicate that hardly any of the students who studied in university or polytechnic drama departments have yet found their way into television as directors. Most of those who had been through one of these had come from Bristol University's film and television postgraduate course. Even more than with theatre directors, television directing seems to be something you grow into. 82% of television directors had another related job before they reached this position.

f. Acting Experience

A quarter of all television drama directors have acted professionally at some time, but 65% have had no experience of acting at all, which suggests that the training directors have had is aimed at the specific technical requirements of the job, and that the experience of acting is not an important factor.

g. Types of Directing Experience

Understandably, a low proportion of television directors had worked in theatre, although one in ten had worked for a regional repertory company at some stage. The breakdown is:

Regional repertory:	10%	National companies:	4%
Fringe:	8%	Community theatre:	2%
Drama school:	7%	Other student drama:	2%
West End:	6%	Middle-scale touring:	2%
Small-scale touring:	4%	TIE:	2%
Commercial touring:	4%	Mime and dance drama:	0.4%
Amateur:	4%	Opera:	0.9%
Overseas:	4%		

Drama work in television seems to be strongly London-based. 94% of directors had done between one and four of their productions in London.

h. Amount of Work

The timescale in television production is usually much slower than in the theatre, so it is not surprising that very few directors have done more than four television productions in the past three years. 92% have done between one and four productions.

i. Earnings

Employment conditions in television seem much better than in the theatre. For the financial year 1986-87, 62% of directors had 39 or more paid weeks of work. 10% had no paid work. Just over a quarter supported themselves with other related work during the year. Television directors emerge as much better paid overall than theatre directors, no doubt because of the length of their engagement and the considerable difference in minimum levels of pay. Nearly a third of them earned over £30,000.

Gross earnings as a director for the financial year 1986-87 were as follows:

Under	£ 1,000	2%
£ 1,000 - £ 5,000		4%
£ 5,000 - £10,000		4%
£10,000 - £15,000		9%
£15,000 - £20,000		10%
£20,000 - £30,000		29%
Over	£30,000	29%

(12% declined to answer this question)

TABLE 10 - GROSS EARNINGS AS A DIRECTOR

This table, which combines film and television, compares the earning levels with those of theatre directors.

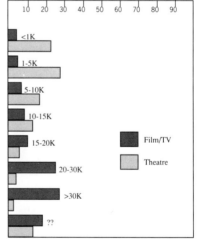

Percentage of respondents

4. Film

The pattern with British film directors differs from that of theatre and television directors. Just over a half are graduates and just over a third have come from a public school. However, most film directors have had no formal director training. The profession is also almost exclusively male.

a. Male/Female Ratio

Taking all ages, 92% are male; 8% female.

b. Age and Experience

As with television it is a profession in which young people are unlikely to make their mark. We heard from no working film directors under the age of

30. Exactly half of the directors were in their 40s; a quarter were in their 30s; 15% were in their 50s; and 11% were over 60. There is further evidence that film directors reach that position comparatively late in life: 37% of them have been working as directors for less than ten years; 34% have directed for between 10 and 20 years; 18% for between 20 and 30 years; and 11% have worked as film directors for more than 30 years.

c. Ethnic Origin

85% were British born and 98% gave their ethnic origin as European.

d. Educational Background

Public school education accounts for 35% of film directors, while 47% went to a grammar school. 23% went to a comprehensive, which is quite a high figure considering that about half of them would have already left school by the time comprehensive education was introduced. 52% of film directors were university graduates, a smaller proportion than in other categories.

e. Formal Training

Surprisingly few film directors have had any formal director training, which suggests that one of the most common ways into the job may have been through other related jobs like editing or working on the camera crew. Only a quarter of directors have been to a film and television school: the first course, at the London Film School, was not established until 1953, and the National Film and Television School did not open until 1971. 5% came through a drama school and 5% came through a university or polytechnic drama department. 63% were without any formal director training at all. Supporting the idea that most directors have grown towards that position through other areas of the film profession, three-quarters of film directors had another related job first.

f. Acting Experience

21% of film directors have acted professionally at some time; 65% have had no experience of acting.

g. Types of Directing Experience

Very few film directors have had any experience of directing in the live theatre. The highest percentage, 3%, was for national theatre companies, West End, fringe, drama school and overseas.

h. Amount of Work

The timescale in film production is even slower than in television. Only 2% of directors have made more than four films in the past three years. Again, almost all this work was London-based.

i. Earnings

As with television, employment opportunities are good, though not as continuous. For the financial year 1986-87, 31% of directors had 39 or more paid weeks of work; 28% had no paid work. Over a quarter supported themselves with other related work during the year.

Film directors are well paid, with nearly a quarter of them earning more than £30,000 although less money seems to be earned than in television. The fact that 26% of film directors declined to answer the question on earnings may mean that the figures are not entirely accurate.

Gross earnings as a director for the financial year 1986-87 were as follows:

Under	£ 1,000	5%
£ 1,000 - £ 5,000		3%
£ 5,000 - £10,000		16%
£10,000 - £15,000		5%
£15,000 - £20,000		8%
£20,000 - £30,000		15%
Over	£30,000	23%

5. Radio

As in the case of opera directors, we were working from a very small sample. Most of the radio directors we heard from were employed by the BBC. The trend is repeated: a male, European graduate.

a. Male/Female Ratio

70% of radio directors are male; 30% female.

b. Age and Experience

Radio tends to be dominated by mature directors. Half of them are in their 40s and 20% are over 50. Another 20% are in their 30s and 10% are under 30. Our figures suggest that directors stay with radio for quite a long time. Although no one we heard from has more than 30 years' experience, 40% have been directing for between 20 and 30 years; a third have directed for between 10 and 20 years; and a third have directed for less than 10 years.

c. Ethnic Origin

90% of radio directors were born in Britain and gave their ethnic origin as European.

d. Educational Background

40% of radio directors had a public school education at secondary level and 70% of radio directors are graduates.

e. Formal Training

Half of the radio directors we heard from had some formal training as a director.

f. Experience of Acting

Most radio directors have had some experience of acting. 40% have never acted at any level and 30% have acted professionally.

g. Earnings

Many radio directors have continuous employment and are well paid, which helps explain why the incomes are in the higher range. However, a third of the radio directors we heard from declined to state their income, which affects the accuracy of these figures.

Gross earnings as a director for the financial year 1986-87 were as follows:

Under £ 1,000	nil
£ 1,000 - £ 5,000	nil
£ 5,000 - £10,000	nil
£10,000 - £15,000	20%
£15,000 - £20,000	30%
£20,000 - £30,000	10%
Over £30,000	10%

Chapter III

HOW DIRECTORS ENTERED THE PROFESSION

III

Before we can determine whether and to what extent director training is necessary, it is important to understand precisely how today's directors reached the positions they are in. We need to see where they come from and how they go through the profession.

As the statistics have shown, most of them were not formally trained, yet there can be no doubt that under the conditions that have prevailed so far, some very fine directors have emerged. Of course there has also been a great deal of mediocrity and even outright incompetence. The question is: could directors have been significantly better with proper training?

It is possible that the qualities of Britain's most eminent directors defy formulation. They follow no particular pattern; they each find their own, often idiosyncratic, way towards their goal. But an examination of how some of the most successful directors built their careers will help us identify the qualities that might be developed in any aspiring director.

1. Where Directors Come From

Very broadly, directors come from two main sources: they are either promoted from within the profession, or they come from the outside, usually directly from university.

a. Within the Profession

The advantage of the first way is that directors will almost always have had some professional training in a related area and a good deal of hands-on experience that makes a useful foundation. This is, in part, why in the theatre so many actors have successfully made the transition to directing. They know what other actors want, they have developed an inbuilt sense of what will work on stage and, above all, they have the huge advantage of having worked with many different directors. Inevitably, once someone becomes a director that facility no longer applies.

Theatre directors who have come through stage management have had excellent opportunities to observe directors at work and, of course, their background gives them a clear understanding of lighting and sound. Thus Deborah Warner, who consciously chose this path to directing, found it a huge advantage. She was trained as a stage manager, then worked as a deputy stage manager and later as an administrator before forming her own company, Kick Theatre. "The most useful thing was being a DSM," she recalled. "It's enviable because it's the only person who wins the right to be in the rehearsal room all the time who isn't the director or the actor. I wrote endless letters to Peter Brook to see if I could come and watch his rehearsals, and he very sensibly wrote back and said, 'No you can't because you'd be bored,' which is absolutely true. And I don't let people watch mine, and I'm always feeling guilty about that. So I think you do have to cheat. You have to become a form of DSM. If you can get in there and you've got a function, you disguise your interest."

Max Stafford-Clark also valued his beginning in stage management: "When I left university and started working as an ASM, I suddenly appreciated that everybody was interdependent, whereas, at university, nobody's earning a living at it, therefore everybody can be slightly more individual and really concerned about their own ambitions."

Trevor Nunn's attitudes were influenced by his working as an amateur actor at the age of 14. "I was extremely fortunate to gain that sense so early on that it wasn't a hugely glamorous profession. It was a profession that was to do with a lot of hard work and intelligence and a lot of compromises and sudden thinking-on-the-feet decision-making. There was a toughness that was to do with survival."

In film, as our survey showed, relatively few directors have come to the job through acting: most have worked their way in through some other role in the production team. This gives them a thorough working knowledge of the technicalities of film-making and the techniques of other directors by the time they are in the director's chair themselves.

David Lean began as a number-board boy, then edited and did commentaries. Jack Gold started as a film editor: "I find it very useful with crews if you can suggest something to them technically, or know when they're bullshitting, which is even more important. So coming up through sound and cutting has been a great advantage."

b. The University Factor

By 1963 there were still only three university drama departments in the whole of Britain. This means that most of today's senior directors did not have the chance of studying drama at a university or polytechnic: they were more likely to study English.

Young people coming out of university may have the self-confidence that gives them the necessary leadership skills to be a director, and, if they studied English under a teacher such as F R Leavis at Cambridge, they may have developed a strong feeling for the language of classical texts. What they may lack is a sense of how theatre, film or television actually works. Consequently their enthusiasm when they begin working with actors may be overshadowed by their ignorance of conventions. Often this can be interpreted by the actors, crew or stage management as arrogance or conceit. Even Peter Brook admitted antagonizing his actors unnecessarily when he first started, simply because he had misunderstood the relationship between the actor and the director.

Graduate directors who have not come from drama departments sometimes hit the profession with a jolt. One stage manager, Claire Mason, commented, "In my experience, the directors who have really made me want to leave the business are the assistant directors, who come out of Cambridge and think they are the bee's knees. And I am fed up with other directors telling me it's part of my job to lick them into shape. Most stage managers have had horrendous experiences with young directors."

Oliver Neville, Principal of RADA (Royal Academy of Dramatic Art) was equally critical of young, untrained university directors. ''They are so bloody sharp, they cut themselves,'' he said. ''Respect and listening to older actors is incredibly important.''

Arrogant attitudes among young graduate directors need to be discouraged, but when people are coming from drama departments or other formal courses they have no way of learning the conventions of professional behaviour other than by trial and error. Many directors stressed the importance of life experience. According to Teddy Kiendl, ''One of the most important skills of a director is to be able to tune in to any world very quickly. Now if you've never tuned into any world but the one you grew up in, how the hell are you going to spend a lifetime doing it?''

2. The Oxbridge Factor

A very large proportion of successful middle-aged directors working in the British theatre today studied at Oxford or Cambridge. This applies to a lesser extent to television directors, while relatively few film directors come from this background.

All the following senior directors over 45 attended Oxford or Cambridge:-

Lindsay Anderson	Oxford	Peter Hall	Cambridge
John Barton	Cambridge	Frank Hauser	Oxford
Peter Brook	Oxford	Jonathan Miller	Cambridge
Richard Eyre	Cambridge	Trevor Nunn	Cambridge
William Gaskill	Oxford		

Film and television directors are more likely to have worked their way through other related jobs within the profession, so there is less incidence of a university education. Thus, the university backgrounds of the following prominent film and television directors are:

Richard Attenborough	none (RADA)	Sir David Lean	none
John Boorman	none	Mike Leigh	none (RADA,
Stephen Frears	Cambridge		London Film
Jack Gold	London		School)
Peter Greenaway	none	Christopher Morahan	none
Hugh Hudson	none	Alan Parker	none
Derek Jarman	London (Slade	Nicholas Roeg	none
	School of Fine	Ken Russell	none
	Art)	John Schlesinger	Oxford
Roland Joffe	Manchester	Charles Sturridge	Oxford
Terry Jones	Oxford	Michael Winner	Cambridge

Clearly the Oxbridge tag opened a lot of doors for its bearers, as it has done in other professions. But what was it about Oxford and Cambridge that produced so many fine directors? The Cambridge tradition has been particularly strong. There was a period in the late 1950s and early 1960s that saw an extraordinary flourishing of talent among both actors and directors. The people who swept in on that wave were energetic, enthusiastic, determined and immensely confident. Their efforts at that time have since carried them to the top of the profession, though nothing like it has happened since.

The teachings of F R Leavis were highly influential, also strong was the presence of George Rylands who directed productions in one of the Cambridge University's drama clubs. Rylands had directed Gielgud and Ashcroft in the 1940s and he formed a vital link in a chain of Shakespearean productions that stretched back to William Poel and forward to the consolidating of the Royal Shakespeare Company. John Barton was also an influence at Cambridge. Apart from its literary stimulus, Cambridge had the advantage of several extremely active theatre clubs. As Peter Hall recalled, ''Mostly I used Cambridge to be in a theatre which was extremely cut throat and very busy. I think I directed five plays in the last three terms, which is rather more than you would do in the profession. The thing special about Cambridge was the ADC Theatre, which was run by the students. You could more or less do what you wanted if you got yourself in a position of sufficient power in the undergraduate committees.''

Trevor Nunn described the same Theatre: ''Its finances were supervised by a Cambridge schoolteacher, but everything else was the entire responsibility of the students. Now when in your second year at university you discover that you are actually responsible for running a building and the building has a budget, and you are doing plays because you want to be dynamic and you want to be irreverent and you want to outflank everybody else - but you also want an audience, and you also know that your show has got to come in on budget - then the students themselves had to become responsible about good housekeeping. We didn't realize it at the time. I certainly didn't think, 'hey, what a wonderful training ground this is'.''

Another factor was that in those days several national newspapers carried reviews of Cambridge university productions. Trevor Nunn: ''Because of that there was a sense that you weren't working in the dark, in a backwater. You were working as ambitiously as it was possible to work.'' There is an interesting parallel here if one compares the situation in the regions today and the difficulty regional repertory companies have in drawing national attention to their productions, however stimulating they may be.

For Richard Eyre, Cambridge was like a semi-professional conservatoire, although his experience there was that of an actor, not a director. He was strongly aware that, with the regular presence of London theatre critics, this was very much a professional testing ground. ''All those people actually put much, much more attention and commitment into working in the university theatre than into the reason they were there,'' he said. ''The stakes were rather high and there was terrific cocksureness about the university theatre. We'd regularly do three shows in a term, so you'd come out having done something like 20 shows over three years, and with some good directors."

These comments suggest that it was an unusual set of conjunctions that made Cambridge theatre so influential at that time rather than a mantle of privilege. The theatre there is not as remarkable today. A group of talented and ambitious people were working in a very competitive situation watched over by experts. There was also the strong sense of pragmatism in everything, which reinforces the idea so many directors have expressed on this Enquiry, that you learn to direct by doing it. As Peter Hall noted, "When I came out of Cambridge I was as equipped as one could be for the hurly-burly of professional theatre life. And actually I got my first job within two weeks of leaving Cambridge."

Today in the theatre there seems to be a move away from the Oxbridge network, as student directors explore other places to learn. A list of prominent directors under the age of 45 and their university backgrounds, or otherwise, supports this:

Bill Alexander	Keele	Jude Kelly	Birmingham
Pip Broughton	Cambridge	Barry Kyle	Birmingham
John Caird	Bristol Old Vic Theatre School	Adrian Noble	Bristol
		Di Trevis	Sussex
Tony Clark	Manchester	Paul Unwin	Bristol
Ron Daniels	Theatre Workshop, Sao Paulo	Clare Venables	Manchester
		Jatinder Verma	York/Sussex
Howard Davies	Bristol	Deborah Warner	Central School of Speech and Drama
Declan Donnellan	Cambridge		

3. The Bottleneck

It is a characteristic of some of the best directors that they established themselves very early on. Peter Brook made his first film at 19 and was directing Shakespeare at Stratford by the time he was 21. Peter Hall directed at Stratford when he was 26. Trevor Nunn directed at Stratford when he was 25 and was running the Royal Shakespeare Company at 28. Charles Sturridge directed *Brideshead Revisited* for Granada when he was 28.

Several directors spoke of the pressure on them to succeed at a very early age. Paul Unwin: "There's a very small bottleneck of experience that people have to get to. If they get through it, they're lucky. And it goes like this: they get on one of the [attachment] schemes; if they are lucky, they get to a theatre which is prestigious, and if it's prestigious, they're away. If they don't get through that bottleneck, they can miss the boat entirely."

Peter Lichtenfels supported this: "If you're not a director by 25, then it's too late. If you're not running your first theatre by 31, then it's too late."

While the film industry does not seem to make these demands today (and the absence of young film directors quoted in our survey confirms this), the emphasis on extreme youth is merely exaggerated by schemes like the Regional Theatre Young Director Scheme (RTYDS) which is available only to directors under 26. The BP Young Directors' Scheme, by contrast, is open to those under 35, but even this penalizes many people who wish to become directors in mid-career.

4. The Right Place at the Right Time

Apart from people's efforts to create their own opportunities whatever the circumstances, being in the right place at the right time seems to have played an important part in many careers. It has often accelerated their professional development and pressure-cooked their training. Jack Gold said, "I fell up ladders." He took a job as a trainee studio manager in BBC radio in 1955 at precisely the time when television was expanding. BBC 2 and commercial television were just starting and he was accepted on the first training scheme in the film department. "It was the best possible time," he said. "The expansion was unbelievable. It was like the big bang. I got promoted very, very quickly. I was a trainee for about six months, then I was an assistant, and within weeks I was cutting little films together. Now if I'd have been in the film industry, the chances of becoming an assistant editor that quickly would have been impossible, and the idea of an assistant actually cutting film before five or six years would have been laughed out of court."

With similar haste Christopher Morahan was promoted from floor manager to director in commercial television: "In those days ITV was like the Wild West. For anybody who was actually lucky enough to be in the right place at the right time, they were only too thankful. You would come on and take on this rather lunatic job of directing two half-hour shows a week, live."

At the age of 20 the dance director and choreographer David Bintley joined the Royal Ballet as a dancer just when the company realized that its attempts to develop new choreographic talent had come to nothing. "They suddenly got into a bit of a panic about the future," he said. "I was in the company six months and they said, 'Do a ballet for us.' So really, from that point onwards, anybody who could sling two steps together was given a chance."

Jonathan Miller, recently out of Cambridge and the Footlights Club was performing in *Beyond the Fringe* when he was asked if he would like to direct a play at the Royal Court. "George Devine was rather hard up for a director and said well let's get one of those chaps who's doing this satire stuff to come and do this Osborne play. I had no formal training." There is almost a sense of accident about Alan Ayckbourn's start as a director: "I was asked to do a production because there was no one else around."

Annie Castledine began when she was a mature student at York University. Although already in her 30s, she was able to form her own experimental theatre company there, and through the work of this company she was invited to apply for an Arts Council trainee bursary. ''I didn't wait for anyone to ask me to enter the profession,'' she said. ''I was making theatre and using whoever was around me. It depends on your entrepreneurial instinct. We make our own destiny.''

Deborah Warner had methodically planned her steps to becoming a director. Her own theatre, Kick, collapsed at just the time when RSC (Royal Shakespeare Company) actors had successfully pressured the management to take on more women directors. At the age of 28 she was directing *Titus Andronicus* at Stratford. ''It's not been an uphill struggle for me,'' she admitted, ''because the work has been done by other women before me and I'm extremely lucky.''

Was it luck, or seizing the opportunity? These people all had a hunger which made them ready when the chance came. They could therefore make the best use of the situation.

5. Is The Profession Stacked against Women?

"One male director I was assisting told me that you couldn't direct unless you had a prick." Sue Charman

The past five years have seen a significant increase in the presence of women directors in theatre, both live and recorded. This is most evident on the stage, where more women have reached positions of power as artistic directors of key theatres, for example: Annie Castledine (Derby Playhouse), Jenny Killick (Traverse Theatre) Glen Walford (Liverpool Everyman), Joan Knight (Perth Theatre), Clare Venables (Sheffield Crucible), Nancy Meckler (Shared Experience), Yvonne Brewster (Talawa Theatre Company), Debbie Shewell and Nicky Pallot (The Bush), Jude Kelly (Leeds Playhouse).

The high proportion of women in training institutions and the statistics from our survey indicate that there will be an even greater increase in women directors, in all categories, over the next decade. At present women account for 29% of theatre directors, 17% of television directors and 8% of film directors. (Our survey showed that 30% of radio directors are women though the sample was relatively small, as it was for opera: it showed that 22% of opera directors are female. The true proportions could be much lower.)

If these figures seem low it should be remembered that the National Film and Television School, for instance, takes an equal number of men and women, a trend that is reflected by other film and television schools. Also, the ratio of students in university and polytechnic drama departments is usually twice as many women to men. So more women are coming onto the market than men, and more young women are getting jobs as directors. Our survey supports this. Taking all categories, two thirds of the women at present directing are in their 40s and 50s; only 20% are under 30. Even so, taking all directors under 30, there are now more women working than men: 57% against 43% men.

Certainly women directors are becoming more accepted, but in the meantime, the profession is stacked against them. To take the RTYDS for instance, although there are now more women on that scheme, very few of them in the past have found permanent positions with theatres.

The problem is, as Jack Gold puts it, breaking down attitudes. He pointed out that there were often two-thirds women on a production crew these days, but a bias still persisted. ''I was filming in France recently and I was asked did I mind having a female first assistant. They shouldn't have had to ask that. They wouldn't have asked me if I'd have minded working with a male.''

David Puttnam explained that for two years, although his production company, Enigma, had maintained a policy of positive discrimination towards the development of women directors, ''What actually occurred was a crisis of confidence on the part of the women directors we were encouraging. They seemed to find the type of rejection, which is part and parcel of the feature film business, hard to deal with. Obviously, to an extent, this is also true of some men, but women seemed to find the frequent calls for rewrites, amendments, etc more than they were prepared to deal with. It may well be that the very best of these women found less convoluted opportunities available to them at the BBC or in television generally, and they opted for this career path in preference to the high-profile but very bumpy road which seems to accompany feature film production.''

In television it is significant that more women have found positions as producers and they may eventually be able to encourage more women directors. Some people spoke of women directors in radio as having to compensate for their sex by being all the more assertive, ''making them inclined to walk all over everyone.''

Annie Castledine, who runs Derby Playhouse, says, ''Women have got to be far less afraid of being seen to enable their own. And men have got to see that. I do think women are oppressed in the theatre and I think a lot of it is unconscious oppression, not necessarily intentional. I have been enabled by men. There is not one woman in my theatre history who has so far enabled me. Most members of my board are men.'' Until the composition of boards of directors changes, or at least until their attitudes change, it may be harder for women to get the work. This situation is bound to breed a certain amount of bitterness.

Cases of discrimination are evident. Claire Grove said, ''I think it is harder to get work because that network is not an old-girls network. I resist the idea that it's going on but twice it's happened to me where I could quite specifically say I have been discriminated against. When I went for one particular job I was asked, how do I get on with men? How would I feel directing an all-male play? They would not have asked these questions of a man going for that job. Recently I had a similar experience where I went for a job. I wasn't asked peculiar questions, but I had feed-back from two particular men on this board who felt that I was too aggressive for this job.

III

45

They wouldn't have said that of a man.''

The problem should also be seen in a wider context. As Max Stafford-Clark pointed out, it is not limited to the theatre. ''In positions of executive and managerial responsibility, the odds are stacked against women because of our society, and because of education. So it's not fair to blame the theatre exclusively for that. And there is a kind of confidence that comes from a middle class, male education that's actually very important to being a director. It's not the most important thing, but it's a contributory factor.''

One solution for women has been to create their own opportunities. Increasingly this is happening amongst younger women. Annabel Arden co-founded Théâtre de Complicité. Deborah Warner set up the Kick Theatre Company: ''It was a totally independent company,'' she said. ''I answered to no one and so I had no idea whether the profession was stacked against me or not.''

6. How Professional is the Profession?

"The theatre in this country is amateurish in its attitude. There is a disdain for professionalism." Peter Lichtenfels

It has long been a characteristic of the arts in Britain that gifted individuals have seemingly turned their hand to anything and, if they chose to, have made a good living out of it. The dramatist and architect Sir John Vanbrugh is a fine example.

What must be remembered is that the genius and the mediocre talent have to travel different distances in order to reach the same goal. A few brilliant artists may be able to learn as they go, but the rest need a more substantial training to achieve the same level. The art and craft of directing is one of the most controversial examples of this problem because it is so apparently accessible.

As Peter Brook has written, ''You become a director by calling yourself a director and you then persuade other people that this is true.'' Unlike acting, the field is wide open to anyone with the urge and the belief in themselves. And the validity of this attitude is widely tolerated. Actors will happily talk of 'turning their hand to a bit of directing,' but, as some directors have pointed out, there would be an outcry if directors turned their hand to a bit of acting.

Most directors will give credit to one or two key individuals who may have influenced them, but on the whole they feel they have had little help. And if they have succeeded, it is largely due to their own efforts. They saw what they wanted and made their opportunities. They emphasize learning rather than being taught.

But the paths were not easy. Because there is no tradition of directorial culture in Britain, as there is in the Soviet Union or Eastern Germany, directors have been left to find their own solutions as best they can. So there is an enormous reliance on individual talent. As Peter Hall said, "To be perfectly blunt, I think I felt about five years ago, which was when I was 50, that I knew my craft. I wouldn't say I do it well all the time, but I know what I'm aiming at. Pretty horrifying."

On the other hand, the lack of directorial culture could be one of the reasons why the theatre in this country has been, at its best, so lively and so diverse. Jonathan Miller thought it was interesting that the best directors had, in a sense, started their life as amateurs: "I mean amateur in the best sense of the word; that it was an enthusiatic relationship without the stifling effect of some sort of traditional standard of how it should be done."

Those few directors who have had what they regard as a solid training will tend to look on the rest, and the system, with some distrust. Mike Alfreds, who studied directing for four years at Carnegie-Mellon University in the United States, has supported this view: "There's hardly a director working professionally in this country, I would think, who had a proper theatrical training. Very few people have actually studied their craft, their skills. That's why actors have been so neglected by directors in this country."

The crucial point is that most directors, however successful, recognized that the right training would have been a help. Peter Hall: "How much better we might have been had we been properly trained."

III

Part 1 The director

Chapter IV

HOW DIRECTORS DIRECT

IV

It is the opinion of this Enquiry that while there is much to be admired in British theatre, it could be much better. There are extremely talented people working in theatre, film and television, yet their potential is rarely realized. It could be if directors knew their job better: this concerns director training.

If the training of directors is to be effective and useful then we must first be clear about what constitutes good direction. In Britain the richness of the art lies perhaps in the diversity with which it is practised. There is a wide spectrum of directorial approaches making it very difficult to lay down simple rules and formulae.

Why is poor direction so widely tolerated? The problem is that it is not always detectable from the outside: frequently, audiences do not see it, nor do critics.

This chapter will set out to examine the relative strengths and weaknesses of the ways directors work. Time and again the point has been made to the Enquiry that directing is an isolated, lonely profession in which there are few opportunities to see other directors working. Directors' perceptions can provide a valuable insight into the requirements of the job, but the people in the strongest position to comment on strengths and weaknesses are those who work with directors because they experience, at first hand, the range of approaches.

We therefore asked a wide cross section of people who work with directors what they expected from a director and what their experience had been. We then asked directors of all kinds how they worked and what their experience was (Chapter V). This enabled us to determine the essential skills that a director must have, and to what extent these can be taught.

1. The Actor's Experience

"We've got to the point where directors in the theatre are allowed to behave disgracefully." Patrick Malahide

Directors, in whatever media, work in many different ways, and actors are bound to accept this. From the evidence given to the Enquiry, although there was much criticism of the way many directors conduct rehearsals, actors were full of praise and admiration for some of the directors they had worked with.

Whilst there was no one point on which all actors agreed, most felt that directors should have had experience of acting. At the same time, some felt that professional actors made the least exciting directors. There was also a strong feeling that, in the theatre, the job is not finished on the opening night. Directors should not disappear, but should keep in touch with a production as it grows during its run. This is a time when the actors need help and frequently do not get it.

Actors tended to dislike long expositions on the meaning of the play at the first rehearsal, though they expected the director to have done a lot of preparation prior to the rehearsals. Actors with small parts felt they were usually given little help until they asked for it, while the principal actors got most of the attention. There was praise for women directors because then the female roles take on more importance.

Some of the main issues are summarized below. Because many actors and singers have had experience in film and television as well as the stage, their comments to some extent apply to all categories.

a. Actors' Expectations

The views of actors reinforced the idea that as they progress through their career, perfecting their craft, actors are constantly being directed by people of differing degrees of experience and varying talent. After many years in the profession there appears to be a weariness and a growing impatience with poor standards of work. Those who have had highly successful careers have usually worked with the best of directors: they demand and get respect.

Peggy Ashcroft, for instance, was quite happy with most of the directors she had worked with, but her expectations were clear-cut: "There should be, ideally, a tremendous give and take between the actor and the director. A great director knows that every actor is different from every other one and has to be approached in a different way. And if he's a good director, he knows what he can get from an actor, and he gets it out."

IV

The singer, Donald McIntyre, thought that the ability to generate confidence was a tremendous asset in an opera director. He said, "I've seen casts here [Royal Opera House, Covent Garden] for example - at the first rehearsal, you think, this is going to be marvellous. And each rehearsal gets worse because you're not being allowed to do it. You're being restricted."

What most seems to rile actors is any lack of professional skill or craft in a director. Anthony Hopkins expressed this view: "Over the last 25 years, mostly I have had a productive relationship with directors - that is the ones who, either through long experience or with a natural talent for directing, arrive in rehearsal or on a film set thoroughly 'prepared', with a good grasp and concept of the play or film they are about to direct.

"There are those others, however, who show up not only ill-prepared but with what seems to be a total lack of understanding of an actor's job. This lack of understanding then usually manifests itself as chronic anxiety or fear which, in turn, manifests itself in other behaviour patterns such as arrogance and bullying. This is always non-productive. Although some directors swear that this tension produces a creative environment in which to work, I know of no actor or actress who would ever vouch for this theory."

The actor-director relationship has often become so bruised that many actors have become highly selective about which directors they will work with. Several talked about their 'two lists.' Michael Hordern wrote, "...often staggered by the insight and grasp of the play by some directors for whom, or rather with whom, I have worked, I am equally appalled by the sloppiness and lack of homework by others. I have a short-list of directors from whom I would immediately accept a part (I have no faith in my own judgement) and another not so short a list for whom I would never work again.''

In some cases, as with Michael Bryant, the actor's treatment by directors has led to stoical cynicism: ''I think they've only been about for 100 years, not long in the history of the theatre. The fad will probably pass in time. The good ones ensure that you have comfortable clothes to work in and a bit of light to act in, the bad ones don't. I've seen a lot of good plays ruined by directors, but very few improved by them.''

What is most extraordinary is the strength of feeling many actors have about the incompetence of some directors. Glenda Jackson: ''I have worked with so few directors worthy of the name that I don't think I have sufficient experience to help the Enquiry. I have worked with a great many who have no right to the name of director - my experience of them could fill a book.''

b. The Feeling for Language

Actors with strong experience of classical theatre were deeply worried about the declining ability of younger directors to appreciate good verse-speaking. This is an issue that has implications for actor-training as well as director training and it will be taken up later in this chapter.

Peggy Ashcroft was one of those who thought that the appreciation of language had declined following a reaction against an over-rhetorical manner of speaking Shakespeare on stage. ''It went right down under, when almost to be heard was an insult. And you can't do the great classical plays without having an appreciation of language. Of course it's partly the influence of films and television. It's 'small is beautiful.'''

The ability to speak classical texts well has been related to the Cambridge tradition and it was felt that that source is in danger of drying up. Judi Dench owed her skill in this to her experience of working with John Barton, Trevor Nunn and Peter Hall. She implied that they were the only directors working today who were able to pass this on. ''That's what Peter Hall is passionate about,'' she said. ''Passing on the thing of being able to speak the verse. Because if it goes by the wayside, then it's going to take somebody else to rediscover it again. The thing about it is you never, never, never run out of breath.''

c. Working with People

"If you haven't got a sense of humour and if you haven't got a sense of compassion, I don't think you should be a director." Judi Dench

One of the most serious problems, from the actor's point of view, is the lack of ability among so many directors to create a productive atmosphere in rehearsals. Obviously this is one of the hardest things to train people for, but repeatedly actors talked of directors approaching the rehearsal as if it were a contest or a battle of wills.

Liz McKechnie found that too much face-saving got in the way of honesty and good faith in the rehearsal room. "I have seen so many of these power games. I've seen people reduced to tears by some bumbling berk of a director who is only exercising his own inadequacies on this person. And then all that person gets is that they are not employed by that director again."

Whilst there can be no formula for communicating with actors (and others involved in a production), trainee directors must be made aware of the fine line between creative provocation and destructive abuse. Often the timing, or phrasing, or weight of an instruction can make all the difference.

Peter Copley described two different approaches: "Long ago I was directed by Edith Evans who had a brief era when she saw herself as a lighthouse to guide young actors: she had much trouble with me, finally despaired, groaned curiously and said 'All right then, empty your mind of everything, and let me fill it for you.' I withered from that moment.

"Even longer ago I was Young Siward in a *Macbeth* directed by Tyrone Guthrie. I took this small part most seriously and thought much about it: finally I got together the courage to ask Tony how I should play it. He said, scarcely pausing as he strode across the stage, 'Shining young knight in armour, get on with it, Peter dear.' Wonderful - the one line direction. He never needed to say another thing."

IV

Actors repeatedly described the lack of respect they felt from directors. "We've got so bogged down with the idea of the director as God and boss rather than as an enabler and facilitator," said Alison Skilbeck. "If I am an actor I feel sometimes as if half my brain has been chopped off."

No doubt the abrasiveness and lack of respect from directors are not maliciously intended. Underlying the communications problem is the fact that most directors are probably not even aware of this side of themselves.

Perhaps many directors are simply unfortunate in that they do not naturally generate confidence and energy. Whether that can be taught is questionable. As Judi Dench said, "There are some television directors of whom you think, I'm not going to be able to do any of this."

Communicating well is not always a matter of the words that are used. It can often be what is not said. And here we come back to the intangibles that are difficult to teach. Donald McIntyre thought it was a special quality or attitude that rubbed off on the performers. "It's like conductors," he said. "The more they verbalize, the less they've got to offer." He recalled singing in a production of *Fidelio* which Otto Klemperer was both conducting and directing. "He didn't talk about all those wider issues. He used to just sit there and - nothing. The only thing that he ever said was, 'I will not have acting!' And he got a tremendous amount out of everyone. Don't ask me how he did it, but it rubs off."

d. Problems of Power

Many theatre workers, particularly in experimental or alternative theatre, look with disdain at an hierarchical system that hinders rather than helps the possibilities of development in the theatre. The question of the power of the director is crucial and it is the issue that most worried actors. It recurred throughout the Enquiry. As every actor knows, this is most likely to manifest itself when the director is least secure. It takes a great deal of confidence and magnanimity to be able to say in a rehearsal, 'I don't know what the answer is here'. The pressure always to have answers has led to much abuse of the role of director and much dishonesty.

Part of the problem is that there is no clearly defined code of conduct for the actor and the director (the stage manager probably has a much more clear-cut relationship with the director). The Equity contract states that an actor must "play the part as directed," which leaves the road wide open for the director. As Anne Dennis pointed out, this divisiveness "results in a real lack of generosity between the actor and director which forces them into either non-productive conflict or non-creative submissiveness."

A large number of actors felt intimidated by the power that is vested in directors. At the same time, some actors found that when they themselves came to direct, power was unwittingly exercised in rehearsals and they could not always detect this for themselves. Charles Lewsen recalled directing a production as an undergraduate: "Afterwards someone in the cast said to me, 'We always knew when you weren't pleased with us, because you would clear your throat.'"

But as several people pointed out, if actors can be so intimidated, there is also complicity on their part that they let this happen. The position of the director as god and boss is implicitly accepted. Once more this reflects on the training of actors. As Janet Suzman suggested, there may be something in the training of actors that pushes them towards believing that the director is the last word. She described a film she had worked on "which was an odd experience: a once famous Hollywood star behaved with the utmost deference to the extremely bad director, because her training had encouraged that attitude at all stages."

Part of the problem lies in the dual role of the director as rehearsal leader and employer. There can be no doubt that the employer-role of directors is a great inhibitor to actors. As a consequence, many actors are disinclined to speak out for fear of reprisals. As James Ross, a stage manager, said, "I think a lot of actors nowadays are frightened to argue with directors, because they cast. They have the money, and if you argue, it's 'She's a bloody nuisance, just don't bring her back next season.' And I know one or two actors who haven't been invited back because they have been labelled."

At its extreme the situation may even partly determine the kind of actors who get the work. Mary Cunningham: "What we've got in this country is a situation where directors are bosses: they pick actors who then behave themselves so that they'll get into the next production.''

As a director Richard Eyre agreed that there were well justified frustrations from actors. ''Sometimes when you sit down with a group of actors and hear them talking about directors, it's like hearing the camp guards of Buchenwald being discussed and it's sort of terrifying.''

If the theatre is to be truly exciting there must be risk-taking on both sides. This calls for directors to be as open and vulnerable as they expect actors to be.

e. A Lack of Method

One of the most frustrating experiences for actors is working with directors who do not really know what they are doing, who have no plan, and who are not able to use the rehearsal time constructively. This is not to say that rehearsals should be rigidly planned: many of the finest directors have grown from early rigidity towards an approach where they can respond increasingly to what the actors bring to a rehearsal. But to be able to improvise to this extent calls for immense skill and preparation. That is where role-models are a danger. As Patrick Malahide suggested, ''In a sense Peter Brook is part of the problem because he's the exception rather than the rule. What worries me is that for every Peter Brook there are 99 others who assume that they are able to move into the profession with the same degree of confidence.''

IV

On the other hand there are some directors whom actors find terribly good in rehearsals, but terribly bad at getting it all on stage. Good training should make young directors aware of the choices of approach that they have, not just in theory, but by thorough application in rehearsal. From there they can eventually go on to find a way of their own, because originality is essential if the theatre is to be lively.

The development of taste and a sense of self-discipline are vital in a director if rehearsals are going to hold together. Jean Perkins described what often goes wrong. ''One director was terribly inspiring at the read-through with his interpretation of the text, but we then spent two out of three weeks blocking and the final week putting in cheap bits of business. The finished product was more like a freshers' revue than his original vision of the piece. Even worse, he was pleased with it and didn't seem to notice that none of his points could possibly be grasped by the audience.''

There have even been occasions, at the highest levels, when productions have collapsed in rehearsal due to the director's inability to communicate with the cast, or through sheer lack of skill. Alex McCrindle: ''I was working with a young director and the actors had to take over and direct it because he was totally incompetent.''

f. A Sense of Challenge and Danger

"I think I could be stretched. I still enjoy acting, but I don't find it exciting."
Simon Molloy

Peter Hall thought part of a director's job was to ask the impossible of an
actor. But to do this with satisfaction to both sides is a mark of greatness.
Several actors drew attention to Tyrone Guthrie's analogy with the conductor
Sir Thomas Beecham. A musician had said of Beecham, "It isn't that he
makes you play as well as you can. He makes you play better than you knew
you could."

All good actors love to be challenged and stretched because it makes them
feel they are getting the best out of themselves. This is another one of those
intangibles that is difficult to teach directors. The best directors have
developed their own personal approach that they would be reluctant or unable
to formularize. Directors without talent are more likely to have developed a
set of empty tricks.

Every actor is vulnerable and needs the stimulus and challenge of a sensitive,
demanding director. A director should never underestimate what an actor can
do or give to a production. Many directors are too easily satisfied, the finest
will ask for more and more from an actor.

A common weakness is that directors will level off at a certain point in the
work and be incapable of going further, simply because they do not know
how to use the rehearsal time to the best advantage. It is, however, dangerous
to suggest a formula. There are times in the rehearsal period when a play
might benefit most from a series of run-throughs, just as there are times when
prolonged improvisation gets the actors nowhere.

The opposite of the director who craves for power is the director in awe of the
actor, which is just as dangerous. Famous actors can give poor performances
because the director has pandered to them or is too polite to tell them where
they are going wrong. "Very often the most eminent people need a slap on the
wrist," said Janet Suzman.

Good training could instill attitudes of integrity and thoroughness in the work
of directors, which would help them to work with actors in a climate of
mutual respect. Unfortunately, this is rarely the case.

g. The Safe Generation

"The new directors coming on don't seem to me to be dangerous,
because they can't afford to be." Mary Cunningham

It is always on the young generation of directors, writers and actors that the
future of the theatre depends. A wave of exciting directors, like the group that
came out of Cambridge in the late 1950s and early 1960s is, as we have seen,
due to historical accident as much as anything. Training alone could not
reproduce that. The importance of this group is that these directors have since
reached positions of power, steering the theatre through the 1970s and 1980s.

It is unwise to slip into the nostalgic view that today's young directors are not a patch on the prodigies of the past. Genuine craft takes decades to learn. So we should not confuse Trevor Nunn or Peter Brook today with the fledgling directors they were when they first entered the profession, making their mistakes along with the rest. And as we have seen, these people are the exceptions anyway.

What training can do is to help young directors side-step a lot of the painful trial and error by giving them a solid starting point from which, if they wish, they can depart. Actors who have been through rigorous professional training themselves are disturbed by the fact that a young graduate can come out of university, fully-fledged and direct plays with no experience of working in theatre at all.

What is more disturbing, and it was a sentiment expressed by directors as much as actors, is that the right to fail is rapidly being eroded. The economic strictures under which theatre companies now operate, and their increasing dependence on market forces, point directors towards playing it safe. And safe theatre is dead theatre. This is one of the hidden costs of policies which value financial more than artistic success. There is a delayed action effect here: one day we will wake up and ask why the theatre is no longer exciting.

IV

All this means that young directors, trained or otherwise, are coming into a depressed state of the art. A blandness pervades, and in these conditions it is hard for them to feel adventurous. Many of the student directors we spoke to revealed a distinct lack of energy and drive. It is therefore not surprising that actors, particularly in the regions, should have expressed concern about the overall quality of young directors. This presages a dull period of theatre.

h. Working in Mime and Physical Theatre

Some of the most innovative direction over the past decade has come not from the text-based theatre but from the area of mime, visual theatre and physical theatre. Although this work was initially of minority interest, its rapidly expanding audience has, in recent years, been matched by significant increases in funding. Consequently, performers like David Glass and Nola Rae, or companies like Théâtre de Complicité, Trestle Theatre and Forced Entertainment are beginning to avoid tiny theatres in order to focus on middle-scale venues. But how far can they go under present conditions?

Unfortunately, the vitality of much of this work is marred by poor direction. The problem is exacerbated when inexperienced directors try to cope with the technical demands of staging productions in larger theatres. So a vicious circle is set up in which the presentation looks shoddy and amateurish, thereby condemning the performers to return to the ghetto.

At the heart of the problem is the fact that very few British directors understand this kind of work or feel much sympathy with it. As David Glass said, ''They may have a very good intellectual understanding of the processes but they can't work physically with actors. Whereas, if you work with someone like Carlo Boso (director of the Venetian group, Tag Teatro), he has an absolute understanding of what is happening physically on stage and what the audience will respond to. He gives you directions through the physical sense, not through the intellectual sense.''

What happens in mime and physical theatre is that performers tend to recruit directors from their peer group. For established performers this can be very frustrating because they are not challenged or stretched artistically. ''I want people who have enormous experience,'' says Glass. ''I don't want people for whom this is their first or second directing experience.''

There are two main solutions: either experienced directors who have an interest in this area are trained to understand how to work in a more visual and physical way, or the mime and physical theatre performers are trained in directing skills. The latter seems to be the more satisfactory solution, but arguably it could take just as long as it takes to train any other director. More short courses, such as the two-week directing workshop Mike Alfreds gave for the 1986 British Summer School of Mime Theatre, would be of great value as an interim solution. But there can be no escaping the fact that mime theatre and physical theatre urgently need well-trained directors if they are to move closer to the mainstream.

i. Working in Opera

Of all the theatre forms opera seems to be the one most in need of reform. The conditions under which operas are staged are frequently unsatisfactory for all concerned, yet almost everyone tolerates them. The usual reaction is that that is the way opera is and no one is going to change it. Singers are dissatisfied because the performer's needs are often subordinated to production concepts. Because the design elements in opera tend to be bolder than in spoken theatre, the singer is very often placed in situations where it is difficult to hear the orchestra or to see the conductor - such as singing from behind a gauze - or they are asked to cope with the acoustic problems of singing in a set lined with sound-absorbent materials.

According to Donald McIntyre, the biggest mistake repeatedly made in opera is that directors put what the audience is supposed to see and hear in a position where they cannot see and hear it. He described one set where there was thick carpet up the walls. ''No matter how great the voice is, you're not going to survive in those conditions,'' he said. ''In opera, the stage is part of the instrument. The voice actually doesn't go anywhere, unless it's got the right sort of backing. It's amazing how many quite experienced directors haven't thought of things like that. If they had, their shows would be so much better.''

Of course these problems are not restricted to opera, but they could almost certainly be eliminated if opera directors were trained to think more intelligently about design and the use of the stage space.

Standards of safety are sometimes abused, not only in opera, but in all media. Richard Duployen described an English National Opera (ENO) staff director who wanted to introduce some dangerous 'business' involving throwing bottles: ''He cut himself on a bottle and had to change to using safe (unbreakable) bottles.''

j. Working with Film and Television Directors

"When I first started, people said, 'are you an actor or do you work in films?' " Richard Attenborough

Although, as will be seen later, the training of television directors neglects working with actors in favour of the obvious technical demands of the job, there was an awareness among actors that television directors tend to have a professionalism that stage directors do not always possess.

Actors tended to feel that, given time and money, and the emphasis on getting the technical things right, the balance is more satisfactory. This might be partly because of the conditions of television production which necessitate getting on with the job. And as with film, big budgets and tight schedules concentrate the mind.

IV

Perhaps because of the lack of knowledge about acting on the part of many television directors, there is more room for mutual respect in a highly professional atmosphere. Patrick Malahide made this comparison: ''I think if you were to measure the bullshit quota, it would be much higher in the theatre than it would be in film and television. I think that in film and television it is much less easy for a director to get away with things, because he knows that in film and television you rely on professionals like cameramen.

''TV directors spend 80% of their time absorbing the technology. To a certain extent that attitude carries through into their professional work. I'm not saying that it's 100% a good thing, but at least it gives you space to get on with your job.''

However, it was noted that because television directors are primarily concerned with the technical requirements of a production, their attention is directed more to the edge of the screen than to the centre of it: if another camera or the microphone comes into shot, then the director is in trouble. To prove this, one actor, playing a Vietnam soldier naked to the waist, put on three strings of pearls and the director did not notice.

Of course, different actors demand different things. While some may appreciate space, others will want more explicit guidance, and directors must recognize that. There will also be occasions in film and television productions when large numbers of extras are employed. A sensitive and well organized director can, even under the pressure of time, go a long way towards making the experience more satisfactory for everyone.

It should also be noted that standards of acting, and of directors working with actors, have improved considerably in the past 20 or 30 years. As Richard

Attenborough, who began as an actor, recalled, "You must understand, historically, that acting for the films in the United Kingdom was beyond the pale. When I began after the War, the majority of directors I worked for hadn't a remote idea of how to talk to you."

2. The Playwright's Experience

Most of the writers we heard from were dissatisfied with their status in both live and recorded drama and frustrated by the way directors often treated them. Like the actors they also acknowledged that they had worked with helpful and unhelpful directors. There was an overwhelming feeling that directors should have some experience of writing plays as part of their training, even if it was only to develop a scene through various drafts. It was also emphasized that they should be expected to read a great number of plays, both classical and modern.

Most of the dissatisfaction centres on the fact that the relationship between the writer and the director is haphazard and undefined.

a. A Sense of Protocol

"There's a peculiar absence of any of us knowing exactly how to behave."
Nicholas Wright

The relationship between the writer and the director is every bit as sensitive as that between the actor and the director. It calls for tact, understanding and a sense of friendship. When these elements are not present, a wall of suspicion comes up and resentment grows. At its extreme, the playwright begins to feel alienated, as Edward Bond wrote: "The director has become an obstruction. His role as manipulator makes him a dictator. I say manipulation because in effect that's what happens. At the Royal Court the directors now simply tell writers how to write plays. They get the writer to solve problems for them - instead of presenting them with the problems of the street and the city."

According to many of the writers we heard from, all too few directors are aware of how personal a play is to its writer. Sheila Yeger: "Directors can be dangerous when they forget that a text is an exposure of a writer's psyche. And they go walking over it in their hobnail boots, very insensitive to what it's meant to that writer to put it down on paper. The good director is extremely aware of that, and where things are not working in a theatrical sense, approaches it in a very cautious manner. The insensitive director can actually devastate the writer."

Some of the most fruitful experiences have come from a working relationship with one particular director, where mutual respect grows over a long period. In his youth Arnold Wesker had such a relationship with John Dexter. "A lot of it must depend on the shared understanding," he said. "Dexter in those early days was only ever concerned to direct the play I had written. The problem has developed that directors - on the Continent and elsewhere - do want to impose, which is why they haven't got as many playwrights as we've got."

In so many cases the relationship seems to be based on ignorance and misunderstanding, which leads writers to feel persecuted. David Edgar believed there was an unspoken attitude that playwrights were not regarded as being theatre professionals. ''From that comes the attitude of them being brilliant but precocious 12-year-olds that need to be treated as infants,'' he said. ''I think that some element of a training course could indicate how difficult writing is and how technical writing is.''

The crux of the problem is that it has never been defined how a director should work with a writer. Negotiations over the past decade have meant that the writer now has a contractual right to be in the rehearsal room, albeit unpaid, but what actually happens in that room between the director and writer varies enormously. David Edgar: ''It has always struck me that there is a terrible lack of protocol in the relationship between the playwright and the director. I think it would be very interesting to develop, via a training course, the notion of what is commonly expected practice.''

IV

This idea was also put forward by Frances McNeil who had experienced similar problems in community theatre and radio drama: ''There could be a code of practice of what a writer expects from the director. Some of the things seem so obvious - like discussing the text with the writer beforehand.''

By contrast, directors in the United States may have had the advantage of a particular method instilled during their training. Anthony Minghella recalled a recent experience with a director in America. ''At the very first meeting he asked me to read the play to him. We spent the entire day, and after each scene he gave me the opportunity to say what I wanted from it, what I thought it was about, where its focus lay. And it was wonderful. Apart from anything else, as a practice, it establishes some common ground and vocabulary. Then it's much harder, at a later date, to resort to blaming the director for misunderstanding you if things go wrong!''

b. Who Directs New Plays?

"I was talking to a director at the RSC who has never done a new play, and when I asked him why, he said none of them were as good as the old ones." James Pettifer

Most older directors would seem to regard their artistic peak as being a satisfying production of a Shakespeare play - if they ever have the chance to do one. Established directors, like Max Stafford-Clark, who have a commitment to new writing are comparatively rare. As a result, in most companies the new play slot is usually given to a junior director. On the fringe and in the alternative theatre, it has long been accepted that new writers go hand in hand with new directors, trying to prove themselves together.

What is overlooked is that an unperformed script places special demands on a director that are quite different from an established classic, or even a second production of a new play. There may be extensive rewriting and the rehearsal room atmosphere may be less secure as actors cope with learning new sections of text at late notice.

As Arnold Wesker said, "In a new play an author is speaking for the first time and it is my belief that everyone connected with that production has a moral responsibility to ensure that this voice is heard and understood as the author's and no one else's. If someone else's voice gets in the way then it becomes an act of censorship."

One playwright had a play accepted for production in one of the RSC's Early Stages seasons. The work was taken on by one of the Company's assistant directors, "an enthusiastic but inexperienced 27-year-old." After several clashes over the treatment of her script, she withdrew the play. "The whole event was unpleasant, and I believe unnecessary," she said. "I believe the fault lay with the administration of the RSC who encourages its younger employees to experiment, but provides no training, no authority or co-ordinator (and no resources)."

Such situations could be ameliorated with good training prior to trainee directors coming to a theatre on attachment. Any training course should make clear the great responsibility that a director of new work bears. As Alan Drury pointed out, "If a director does a rotten production of *Coriolanus,* people say 'Oh well there'll be another production of *Coriolanus* - like the 97 bus - along soon.' Whereas if you get a dreadful world première production of a new play, that play then usually completely disappears."

c. A Sense of Mise-en-scène

"There is a whole generation of younger directors who have very little sense of theatre." Jo Anderson

While training should help directors understand how to fulfill the textual needs of a new play, the balance between what the audience hears and what it sees should not be neglected. This is one reason why it is essential for young directors to see as much theatre as possible, so that there is a familiarity with the literature on stage, not just on the page, and a developing sense of taste.

Pam Gems found other writers in agreement when she said of directors, "You can have these very literate conversations with a director, but they have no idea of mise-en-scène. They have no idea of three-dimensionality. I could name you directors who have no talent in that direction. They are good scholars, their meaning is clear, but it isn't the play. It's a play-reading of the play."

d. Whose Play is it Anyway?

Several of the writers we spoke with were worried about their changing role in theatre. Since the increase in devised work, particularly among community and TIE groups, the social context has begun to change and companies are having more of a say in determining the content of a new play they are commissioning. This also happens to some extent when larger theatre companies commission an adaptation. All this puts more demands on the skills of the director to work with a writer.

For the process of briefing a writer who is commissioned, and for the developmental stage between the first draft and the first rehearsal, there is no protocol. Yet this is becoming an increasingly important element in the relationship between the writer and the director.

Another question is the extent to which the director should intervene over the content of a play. As Nicholas Wright put it, ''There is a danger of institutionalizing the director as an authority on what the play or text finally ought to be like.''

In cases where directors have been extensively involved in the rewriting of a play, the fundamental question of ownership becomes ambiguous. David Edgar: ''Something coming up at the moment, which is quite nerve-racking, is the idea of directors considering that they have some rights over the script on the grounds of what's changed in rehearsal and what contribution they've made.''

IV

e. The Playwright as Director

''Writers who want to direct their own plays should direct them.''
Arnold Wesker

It has to be said that this seems to throw the whole question of director training upside down: if writers start directing their plays, then should not they too be subjected to the demand for thorough training before they are let loose on actors, stage managers and so forth?

Nevertheless, a significant number of leading playwrights have made it a rule to direct their own work, which takes us back to Aeschylus, Molière and Shakespeare. Alan Ayckbourn, Steven Berkoff, Edward Bond, David Hare and Harold Pinter, to name a few, have all directed their own plays, or film scripts, at the most prestigious levels. Some of them have even directed each other's work, and with considerable success. A few of them, like Ayckbourn, have as much professional theatre background as any director in the business. And if they feel they have the ability, then who better to look after their plays?

At the root of this is the feeling that many playwrights have been bruised once too often. James Pettifer: ''I should think most people who've had three or four plays done would have had one very bad experience on average. That's why I think people instinctively would like sometimes to direct their own work. There is always that awful memory somewhere: is it going to happen to me again?''

f. Working in Film and Television

"Directors in film actually believe that writers should reach a certain point and then disappear." Olwen Wymark

Most writers who had experience of working in film found their relationships with directors limited and unsatisfactory, although the writer/director relationship in television was generally agreed to be more harmonious. This may be partly due to the status of directors in the television industry. As Anthony Minghella pointed out, ''In television the director is always an employee.''

Most of the concern centred on the procedure whereby writers had less and less control over their work. This was seen as undermining the contribution of the writer to the creative richness of the final product. It was most strongly felt in film, where the director as auteur was difficult for writers to accept.

As Alan Drury explained, the values are reflected in the contractual procedures. ''The film, as we know, is the only medium in this country where they actually buy the copyright from you and they can do what they like with it. Whereas in television, radio and on the stage, you release the copyright for a certain amount of time to the organization that's going to put it on; which means to some extent you have, apparently, some rights over it. Increasingly in film the director thinks it is his project: you are like a cameraman or a sound man, supplying one creative aspect.''

The point was also raised that writers are kept away at some of the most crucial moments - not actually the shooting or the recording. In radio, television and film the most crucial place is felt to be the editing, which can totally change the meaning of the piece: writers are not normally allowed into that.

On these issues it is relevant to note the producer's perspective. David Puttnam believes that ''99 times out of 100 the presence of a writer *on the set* is a liability rather than an asset. At a certain moment, when the director isn't the writer of the piece, the writer has to be prised away from the material and the director allowed a clear run. It may well be a good idea to invite the writer to see the early rushes of the film, but once the tone has been set I would advise that the writer is reinvolved only if it comes to a specific issue of problem-solving as opposed to general opinion.''

Given that the conditions of working may not be able to be changed, it is crucial that directors learn how to communicate with writers, just as they must communicate with actors.

3. The Designer's Experience

Discussions with a number of designers revealed that, as with playwrights, there is no protocol to guide the director and the designer. How a director briefs a designer and how they work together after that varies from individual to individual.

It appears that a large number of directors do not adequately appreciate the full potential of a designer's contribution to the production. Consequently the relationship has often been fraught with misunderstandings, conflicts and lack of communication, usually provoked by the director's inability to brief the designer coherently in the first place.

a. Learning to Work Together

"Directors have a very bad start in life, because they have to develop their skills in practice." Alison Chitty

Almost every designer we heard from believed that directors, if they are to work effectively, should have designed a production at least to model and costume-drawing stage. This was the only way they would understand the processes involved. Design experience should be an important component of any training course. Informal talks between trainee directors and practising designers are also recommended as a way of ironing out future misunderstandings. When directors lack training, designers suffer enormously. Inexperienced directors, who have not yet formulated a productive way of working with designers, cause considerable frustration.

IV

Although design may be included on most directing courses, the question of protocol deserves careful thought. As Christopher Baugh said, "Young directors and designers do not have a clear idea about: what they might expect from each other and how they each might work; and how to begin establishing a working relationship between themselves and within a company of other creative contributors. How do they conduct their first working meeting?"

The problem is exacerbated by the fact that directors have to develop their skills through doing, which means practising on other people, often with disastrous results. As Alison Chitty pointed out, "If this was done by a brain surgeon, or an airline pilot, one wouldn't think it was a particularly brilliant way of going about things."

b. Left out in the Cold

"Designers also need encouragement - not at a first night party, but during the fit-up or production week." Juliet Watkinson

Once the rehearsal period starts it is important for directors to maintain their relationship with the designer. Designers expressed the feeling of exclusion and redundancy as a creative contributor once the director has completely taken over by the momentum and pressures of the rehearsals. As both become involved with their own problems, it is very easy to lose sight of the support and reassurance they should be giving one another. Battles of will arise over minor features of the set and costumes, and misunderstandings grow when the director and designer are unable to find the time to talk through problems that arise.

As Juliet Watkinson said, "Directors usually seem aware of the pressures on actors, but are less aware of how scared, stressed, physically exhausted and 'lonely' a good designer can feel."

c. Thinking Visually

Playwrights spoke of directors lacking a sense of mise-en-scène. Designers were aware of directors lacking the ability to think in images. The visual possibilities of a production are often not explored, while so much attention goes into the speaking of the text. This is one point where British theatre could be said to differ from the rest of European theatre. In fact, on the Continent, bold designs and exciting visual effects sometimes overtake the actor and the text. The best directors, such as Strehler and Stein, usually get the balance right.

Gregory Smith: "On stage, as in life, 50% of language is visual and directors have that language at their disposal. This is often overlooked through ignorance of what visual language is and what it can do. It is regarded with suspicion and is seen as detracting from, rather than enhancing, spoken language. Directors' fear of visual language and their panic at not being able to use it can be a great hindrance."

4. The Stage Manager's and Technician's Experience

Stage managers and technicians saw a strong need for directors to have a full understanding of the technical aspects of theatre, television and film production if they are to work alongside technical staff in an atmosphere of mutual respect. They should not necessarily be able to perform all the functions themselves, but they should know enough about the resources to be able to understand what can and cannot be achieved.

There was strong criticism of young graduates who come into the profession straight from university without any understanding of what it means to work in theatre, and without any respect for the technical personnel.

British Actors' Equity submitted evidence from its Stage Management Committee. One of its recommendations was that training schemes should be directed not only towards 'under 25s' or 'recent graduates,' but also should give encouragement and opportunity to working theatre people, including stage managers, who wish to direct.

a. A Sense of Practicality

"I've had technicals where directors throw wobblies because they don't understand that with certain sets you can't do 42nd Street changes."
Claire Mason

The Equity submission to the Enquiry gave two examples of the sort of directors who make a stage manager's job more difficult than it should be:

"1. A director who shows little interest in technical matters, so that trying to nag them about press photo-calls, sound plots or wardrobe becomes a daily nightmare for the stage management.

2. A director who sees rehearsals only as an exercise in exploring such things as the meanings within a text, so that the stage management are left trying to comfort and support a cast, facing an approaching first night, without ever having been able to start consolidating their performances."

Training that is devised in consultation with working stage managers would help young and inexperienced directors get the best out of their technical staff. 'Crewing' for each other in drama department productions and in film and television school productions offers a valuable practice for this. However, from what we saw of the facilities on some university courses, the scale of experience here is often confined to that of a small studio theatre with limited means.

One of the great tests of a production is on tour. This is an aspect of theatre where stage managers carry a huge responsibility to make things work, while directors are often absent, or well out of the way. As Sheelagh McCabe suggested, "A good training for directors is to be assistant director on tour."

IV

Practical technical experience is clearly useful to a director. An example was given of the French director, Jean-Louis Barrault, who during a tour to the United States made heavy demands on the lighting staff. Their response was, "Jean-Louis, you can't do this." He climbed a ladder and did it.

b. The Audience

It was stressed that part of a director's concern is communication with the audience, yet this is often neglected. Directors will watch rehearsals from Row G of the stalls and be unaware that an important entrance cannot be seen from the side of the balcony. Furthermore, directors often neglect to find out why the house is empty, how the publicity has gone and where the posters are.

This reinforces the point that a director's job is not finished on the opening night. Awareness of the audience dynamics - why they are coughing in this scene, or not laughing in that one - and responding to the audience's reaction, by making adjustments to the production, can be regarded as a final stage of the rehearsal process. Yet directors, especially in alternative or experimental theatre, will often watch a steady trickle of people making for the door and not bother to find out why they are leaving prematurely or what can be done to improve the production.

c. Working with Television Directors

The opinions of television and film technicians reinforced the view that practical knowledge of the technical aspects is essential. One recommendation was that television trainee directors should spend a minimum of two weeks with the department involved in studio production (sound, vision control, cameras, vision mixing, editing etc) in order to expose them to the problems that a director can create with unreasonable or nonsensical demands. This would also give them a clearer understanding of the resources and facilities available to them in making programmmes.

Nina Weaver, Head of Vision Mixers for HTV, wrote, ''An ability to communicate is perhaps the number one skill required to direct successfully and too little time is spent training in this important skill.'' Speaking of conditions in Welsh television companies, Wally Hazlehurst, Head of Lighting for HTV, expressed the opinion that ''nothing is harder to accept than a programme director who has not done his 'production homework' and uses up technical rehearsal time working out what he is going to do with the production - known in the trade as the 'make it up as you go along' system. You may imagine that this group is in the minority - but let me assure you that this group is very much in the majority.''

Eileen Diss, a production designer who works in feature films, television and theatre, believed that often failings in a director's ability were inherent in the personality and would therefore be difficult to overcome through training. She cited an example of a film director who always made last minute decisions or changes which could cause her problems. But this was, she insisted, the working method of a highly gifted man who even if he were to make life easier for her might very well curtail his creativity in the process.

Two very senior television technicians made surprisingly common observations on preparation and communication:-

Dick Hibberd, a studio supervisior with one of the major ITV companies, has observed every manner of director as they worked on all types of studio television programmes. Some of the attributes of a director he would like to see improved include a sense of timing and priorities. In the complex and pressurized logistics of the TV studio, the ability to pace the production through the schedule is vital to avoid time-wasting and end-of-day panics. He still found many directors failing to communicate what they envisaged. Often the most inventive of directors were unable to explain their very good ideas in any comprehensible manner.

Shirley Coward is a long-serving vision mixer with the BBC: ''Studio time is for the technicians. We also have to rehearse and give a performance. The director and the actors should have done their rehearsing in the rehearsal room.'' She also emphasized that ''simple, concise instructions are required. There is no time, or even need, for ten words when one will do.''

Clearly, the experience of working in the technical departments, if only for a short time, would help television directors to work with technicians in a more realistic way that would help remove the 'them and us' attitude that builds up through lack of mutual understanding.

5. The Specialist's Experience

a. The Voice

"I don't think directors challenge actors enough." Cicely Berry

Understanding the mechanism of the voice and being able to make language come alive are principally the work of the actor. But the actor frequently needs help. It is essential that the director also enters this area and is in complete sympathy with it. Therefore, a practical understanding of voice work is an important part of a director's training, particularly as so many senior actors and directors have expressed concern that the feeling for language is declining in the work of younger directors. The problem is not confined to directors who work on classical plays. A great many young directors in fringe, alternative and experimental theatre are frequently working with actors of limited experience and little training. Those actors above all need guidance and careful direction if they are not to misuse or damage their voices. Not surprisingly, hardly any of these small companies are able to afford to use a voice coach, or even think of it. So, greater reliance is placed on the director to deal with vocal problems.

IV

Even in companies where a voice coach is available, not all directors know how best to use this facility. Cicely Berry, voice coach with the RSC, believed that directors do not know enough about this area and are often defensive. Very few of them realize the possibilities. She said, "A director thinks that to make an actor's voice better he can send them along to me and I will do some exercises with them to strengthen the voice, to open up the range or to make the language sharper - which is all relevant and part of one's job and certainly part of the actor's job.

"But what I find that directors don't realize is the total tie-up between how you use language and acting itself. And so very often they put voice work into a separate compartment. I've realized that if actors are not using their voices particularly well, it is usually because something is not going quite right with the acting. That if the language isn't sharp enough it is because in some way they're not seeing the active use of the language - how it is always provoking a response of some sort." What is worrying, she continued, is that on the whole directors in this country do not know enough about actors' processes. "In America they do. Certainly the old-hand director does. They know about the Method. I'm not saying that I think that is the most wonderful thing, but it is a way of working which has very specific parameters."

b. The Body

"We are producing a set of highly educated men who have no movement sense." Belinda Quirey

Similar problems occur in the director's approach to the physicality of the actor. Many people go for the text at the expense of the body, and only a rare director, like Trevor Nunn or Peter Brook, will bring the two parts together.

The physical work is shared by either movement specialists or choreographers, depending on the needs of the play and the resources of the company. As with the voice coach, most companies can rarely afford a movement specialist, and even when they can, the hours will be severely limited, thereby reducing the possibilities of what can be achieved. Movement work, if it is to be of anything but token value, is slow and needs time. Very few directors are in sympathy with this, or understand its possibilities, which is why the physical aspects of productions are so often unsatisfactory. Notable exceptions are companies like Shared Experience and Cheek By Jowl.

Adequate attention to this area in training could bring about a change of attitudes. The Royal National Theatre and the Royal Shakespeare Company each employ full-time voice coaches, but movement coaches are brought in sporadically according to the needs of a particular director.

Referring to her experience of choreographing early opera, Belinda Quirey found a serious lack of appreciation amongst directors of the ways that performers can express themselves physically. ''The ones who know things academically seem to have no consciousness of rhythm,'' she said. ''The young, fashionable directors are the worst. They think they're bringing emotion and truth to it. They think I'm full of old fuss and theatricality, but that's not so. Emotional truth depends on physical truth.''

Virtually all the choreographers we heard from expressed the same sense of misunderstanding, and many of them were disturbed that directors gave them insufficient time to achieve their work. They were brought in at the last minute and directors were unable to brief them clearly. Again, these defects are based on ignorance and should be rectified at the training stage.

Denni Sayers described ''the kind of director who says 'Oh Christ, it's music, that's your department.' They don't come near you before the dress rehearsal. And then they go 'No, I hate it, it's not what I wanted at all.'

''The choreographer says, 'Well it's taken them four weeks to get this very simple dance. It's going to take me another four weeks to teach them another dance.' And then they say 'Well you can have half an hour before the first preview. Can you change it?' So I think directors in their training should be made to learn a dance routine so they can see how long it really takes.''

6. Other Points of View

a. TIE and Young People's Theatre

Most theatre directors are likely to direct a play for children or young people at some point. Indeed, pantomimes and children's plays provide some of the most reliable box office successes in larger theatres. Our survey showed that 42% of directors had worked in TIE. Yet the status of this work is relatively low. Both the critics and the profession generally regard it as being somehow 'inferior' or 'easy,' something jolly that happens at Christmas, the success of which can be measured by the degree of hysteria in the audience. Consequently directors tend to underestimate the skills it requires - to the chagrin of those who specialize in this area.

According to Penny Casdagli, a writer of plays for children, who has also directed, ''There are various rules that apply to staging work for children that should not need to be 'discovered' afresh by each practitioner but should be organized into training. Some rules are simple. A blackout, which is a common adult device for ending a scene, will make a children's audience scream. If two characters playing adults both sit down and talk to each other on stage the audience may start to talk as well (children seeing adults talking assume they are not talking to them). Other 'rules' are much more sophisticated. For instance, action needs to be organized with an intuitive understanding of the audience's ability to concentrate in spans, and 'release' and 'control' movements incorporated into the play's progress.''

Children's theatre is sometimes performed in formal or studio theatres and is then taken out into the community for performances in schools, libraries, museums, parks and streets. Directors should be wary of underestimating the audience, and should be aware of the effect of the play in a context away from the 'home theatre,' for example in a school.

IV

Alistair Black, Drama Adviser for Hampshire County Council, observed that many directors offered workshops as part of a package of school or theatre production without any idea as to how to work with young children or what kind of work they had been doing in their school prior to the visit: ''In some cases the directors and the company have left schools having managed to disrupt and upset the whole school and expecting the teachers to pick up the pieces.''

b. The Producer and the Editor

Most producers and editors felt that if stage directors came to radio and television it did not matter if they lacked a full grasp of the technology, providing they were prepared to learn.

Ned Chaillet, Script Editor for BBC Radio Drama said, ''There are people who come in on attachment and follow through in a very much trailing situation. Then we get people like Keith Hack coming in very unsure of what they can do, following production after production, talking to technicians, talking about what can be done: learning.''

What is essential is that the director can work well with actors in a climate of give and take. Roger Gregory, a freelance drama producer for BBC Television, had watched many directors at work: ''It seemed constantly to be proved to me that good performances and productions came from preparation that helped the actors explore the play and find their version of it.''

Sue Nott, a television producer, contrasted the two main types of television director: those who have come from theatre, who are stronger on text and the understanding of actors but not always so appreciative of the technical possibilities and problems; and those who have come up via the technical ranks. ''The latter sometimes have very little appreciation of the acting process,'' she said, ''and I certainly feel that access to 'real' actors should be an important part of the training of TV directors. Good directors will always prepare well, whether in theatre or television. The pressures of time tend to be greater in television; rehearsal time is often short, which means that directors tend to expect instant results from actors rather than having the luxury and confidence to look on rehearsals as a time of mutual exploration. This pattern of work can then become habitual so that directors begin to accept the first interpretation all the time, rather than use the full time available with the actors. At the same time, however, the ability to make instant decisions under pressure, while keeping calm, is probably a very important quality to be nurtured in budding TV directors.''

David Rose, Head of Drama for Channel 4, emphasized that because television plays are seldom made under ideal conditions, training is vital to ensure that the limited time available is used to the maximum effect. ''There are a number of directors who really don't know what to do at rehearsals,'' he said. ''Once they've got their shots right, they're happy. And there is, I think, just adequate time under the Equity agreement to rehearse say a 50 minute episode if the director knows how to use that time. I don't know how some very good plays are put on.''

c. The Film Producer

The glamorous aspects of a well-financed career in film-making often lure people into this profession for the wrong reasons. Is it because they simply want the status of being a film director, or do they have something that they passionately want to say through film? Too easily, one can become obsessed with technique at the expense of content.

The producer, David Puttnam said, ''I'd rather that we were using the resources of a film school to teach people who really have something to say, how to say it, than to create careers for people who are extremely ambitious and articulate, but who have nothing to say.'' He also expressed concern that many directors regarded their job as making either a 'commercial' film or an 'artistic' film that had something to say. It was his belief that a director should be setting out to make films that had artistic merit but were entertaining at the same time, and he saw this as one of the main challenges of the business.

On the other hand, Puttnam believes that it is important for directors to have a sound ideology in terms of understanding their role in society. It does not specifically matter whether they see themselves as polemicists or highly commercial interpreters but, ''I do expect directors to understand the nature of their role and to be honest about it. This whole area of directors coming to terms with the role they can fill within society is a lot more important that it's given credit for, and should form part and parcel of their training at film school or within the industry.''

Enumerating his expectations as a producer, David Puttnam thought a director should be conversant with how to break down a script; have a good feeling for how long it was going to take to shoot a given number of scenes; be able to anticipate problems; and have some sense of the nature of a special effect and the different means by which a technical problem could be solved. He also put great value on sensitivity in dealing with other artists - not just actors but also writers and technicians: ''Respect for other people at work is something that is part and parcel of someone's character, but it can also be taught.''

d. The Artistic Director

Concerning practice in the theatre, a final word should come from the employer of directors. Peter Hall spoke as somebody who had employed directors, both for the Royal Shakespeare Company and the Royal National Theatre, for 25 years: ''I have to say that there is an amazing level of incompetence among directors, which could not be tolerated among musicians or actors. Many simply don't know how to do it, they allow it to happen by leaving it to the actors. Of course the same is true in the music profession; there aren't many conductors who can *actually* conduct, for instance. But there is a level of incompetence in directors which you don't find even among the worst conductors - they have had a training.''

IV

Chapter V

THE DIRECTOR'S POINT OF VIEW

V

In discussing how they worked, directors gave their views on a wide variety of topics. Space does not permit all the points raised to be included here: the following represents a selection of views which to some extent answer the issues raised in the previous chapter by the people who work with directors.

1. The Experience of Acting

Almost all actors were convinced that directors should have had some experience of acting, no matter how poor their talent for it. Most theatre directors have acted: according to our survey, just over three-quarters of them have acted professionally at some time. Looking back, they agreed that it was a helpful experience, though many of them did not see it as essential. As Jack Gold put it, ''Sometimes it's not as important to know how to fix it as to know when something needs fixing.''

Mike Leigh expressed the other view: ''The experience of having trained as an actor remains the foundation of my directing work, and I am unshakable in my conviction that it is a must for dramatic directors.''

2. Established Actors Turning to Directing

With the paucity of formal director training courses, the acting profession has long been a major provider of directors. This is a fact that has gone largely unnoticed, probably because it was no more than a stepping stone for directors; an experience belonging to their distant past. Peter Hall, Terry Hands, Richard Eyre, Trevor Nunn, Jonathan Miller and Joan Littlewood all acted, though not all of them professionally.

But when prominent actors cross the line to direct, a question is posed. Do they have a right to poach on someone else's territory? The past few years have seen Judi Dench, Geraldine McEwen, Derek Jacobi, Joan Plowright and Janet Suzman all making high-profile directorial débuts. There can be no denying that these people were in a position to pass on a vast amount of valuable knowledge, and their viewpoint is bound to be refreshing. As Judi Dench said of her production of *Much Ado About Nothing*, ''All I could bring was the fact that I knew the play well - admittedly only from Beatrice's point of view. But I understood the play and I knew the pitfalls of the story.''

Besides, from the cast's point of view, they know that they are working with a skilled professional and can respect that. This is one reason why actor-directors have been so popular. Sheila Hancock: ''I believe actors like working with me (most of them!) because I understand their problems. In all other areas I am woefully untrained and inadequate. It is of course disgraceful that I should presume to be allowed to direct. The only excuse is that others are even less well prepared. At least I can handle actors and they are, after all, the most important ingredient in a successful show.''

The crux of the debate is whether actors should be challenging the very role of the director as an indispensable figure in any production. This has caused much defensiveness because it threatens to undermine the seriousness with which the job is taken. The counter argument is that it is needlessly difficult to stage a play without someone directing it. Peter Hall: "The director as dictator or imposer, I'm very against. I sympathize with actors, but I think the corollary of that is that if you say the director has too much power and you take away the power from the director, you end up creating another form of director."

3. Casting

"I'm a strong believer that the success of a film is 80% in the casting, once the script is right." Jack Gold

Most directors we heard from agreed on the importance of casting and felt that it was a vital skill. Under the old repertory system in the theatre, actors were usually hired for a season during which they played a variety of parts, often demonstrating their versatility. But with the gradual demise of that system, actors are more likely to be hired for single productions and are therefore inclined to be cast more to type. Whether one agrees with this approach or not, the significance is that increasingly directors must be able to cast well.

Nowhere is this more true than in film and television. Richard Attenborough believed in giving meticulous attention to casting over a long period of time because it makes the eventual filming easier and the relationship with the actors more relaxed: "I think one of the most important questions of a director's taste is casting correctly. And therefore by the time I go on the floor, I know those actors reasonably well. I can persuade them that they are the only actor on earth to play that part."

4. Working with Actors

How well, then, do directors work with actors? Curiously, many directors we spoke with felt slightly unsure of how their work was received by actors. They could only do what they knew best. The more confident ones happily took on board a teaching role if that was needed. Some were wary. But almost all of them professed to be at least caring towards actors.

Jonathan Miller expressed the polarity that exists among directors: that you are either very encouraging and affirmative with performers, "or you have a brilliant dictatorial ability which frightens actors into performing wonderfully. I would think I was probably rather sensitive with them. I think I get on with them and encourage them and amuse them. I think there are people who think I'm a dictator and a tyrant, yes. They think, 'he comes with the whole thing pre-set and we've got to work like marionettes inside it.'"

Problems also occur in film-making, where there is often insufficient time to explore fully the actor's processes. Richard Eyre: "A lot of what happens in film is that very skilled actors just do their work and directors just shoot take after take after take, and think that in the end they'll get something from one of those. When they sit in the cutting-room they'll be able to say, 'oh well, that one's better than that one,' and it's ignorance of what actors can do."

For Richard Attenborough, working with actors is the greatest enjoyment of film-making and he prided himself that, whether his films were good or bad, they were always well-acted. "That's what I care about," he said. "I believe that the way in which I can convey what I want to say and what I feel and what I want to express, is fundamentally through the actors, not through the skills of editing and so on."

5. Handling Power

"Well, somebody's got to make up their mind." Jonathan Miller

Clearly, directors hold considerable responsibility and power in working with actors. Few realize how much, which is probably why so many actors are upset by the unequal relationship that they usually find themselves in.

Right from the start Peter Hall was struck by the power of his position: "In my early 20s I worked with some of the greatest people in the British theatre - Ashcroft, Olivier, Charles Laughton - and I was aware very early on that, inexpert as I was, if I said the wrong thing at the wrong time, even to Olivier, I could paralyse him from proper work for days. It's a position of enormous power and you have to really be responsible about it. That's something that could be taught. You can destroy the greatest talent for a considerable period of time."

Some directors agreed that there are cases where power is abused and that actors, especially, have a rough time. Others threw the onus back onto the actors and writers who feel victimized, implying that they should look for solutions rather than accept the status quo. Actors are, after all, free to hire themselves and form actors' companies. In Christopher Morahan's view, "If a writer feels the director is taking on too much power and is rewriting his text without his knowledge, then he should ask for a new director."

6. The Director as Teacher

"The actors should know how to speak. They shouldn't be waiting for the director to teach those things." Peggy Ashcroft

Senior directors from national companies were highly critical of the standard of actor training, which made the rehearsal of classical texts arduous. While admitting that there is a supply of exciting young talent, they found many young actors ungenerous, undisciplined and seriously lacking in craft. The significance of this is that the director's role becomes more heavily a teaching one. Directors resent this because they do not see it as part of their job and it erodes valuable rehearsal time. Richard Eyre said, ''There's virtually no ability to deal with classical text - virtually none. You could be more or less starting from scratch.''

A similar view was expressed by Peter Hall: ''When I started doing *Antony and Cleopatra* at the National two years ago, out of a cast of 38 there were two actors who could speak it on the first day, and 36 actors who didn't know how to do it. And I had to teach it for six weeks before we started rehearsing. But that's not uncommon. I don't think that should be, but it is. I don't think a director's function is to teach. Young actors come out of drama school with an ability to be themselves and sell themselves on television, and to play colloquial scripts which are usually underwritten and not very well written, where the subtext is usually more important then the text. In a sense you can't blame drama schools for doing that because that's how they're going to earn their bread and butter. But then they don't come out with any verbal awareness.'' Maybe the director's expectations of the actor, in both live and recorded drama, is a matter which should be discussed by experienced directors and senior staff at drama schools?

The evidence for a lack of work on verse and language in drama training was extensive, and expressed in the strongest terms. The seriousness of the issue is that, through a lack of training, the majority of directors are unable to take on the necessary teaching role when the moment arises. A vicious circle is set up whereby directors are increasingly deterred from staging classical plays, which in turn means that actors have fewer opportunities of playing in them, and the drama schools, being pragmatic, begin to feel that classical drama is less of a priority.

The idea was also put forward by many directors that, if directors are all-powerful figures, their power is willingly given to them by the actors, who implicitly support the status quo of directorial power. This manifests itself in a lack of readiness to challenge the director. Terry Hands believed that actors should make their demands and their questions known. And they should be prepared to do half of the intellectual work. ''Today you tend to get actors who stand there and say 'paint on me'. You get Ophelias who turn up saying, 'Okay, you tell me why she goes mad'. Whereas they should turn up with 15 reasons why they think she goes mad and only accept a 16th if one of their 15 isn't as good.''

7. Working with Writers

The relationship with writers, from the director's point of view, parallels that with actors. There is even the same pattern of writers taking over and directing their own work. There are varying levels of commitment towards new writing on the part of directors. Some have practically built their reputations on it; others have never worked with a living writer.

In large theatres, the status of new writing is ambiguous, which has led to much resentment on the part of writers. As Terry Hands put it, ''The living writers are very pissed off that, on the whole, they get the junior directors and not the senior ones.'' Such a situation could be improved by director training that gives adequate attention to the demands of working with writers.

The writers' arguments for being involved more closely in the production of the film have been aired in the previous chapter. The response of many directors was that if a producer has brought together a writer and director who can work with each other, the relationship can be harmonious, so long as the boundaries are defined. For example, most directors felt that the writer is not much use on the set. As Jack Gold, who has enjoyed very good working relationships with writers, said, ''Finally, they should either direct or shut up. It's not easy to direct with a writer hovering over your shoulder. It's uncomfortable.'' Richard Attenborough, on the other hand, would work with his writer right up to the shooting and he often had the writer on the set.

8. Directing Opera

Many directors would like to work in opera but are unable to establish the contacts that would enable them to make the transition. Opera was seen by many as a closed world. Unless a well-known theatre director is invited by an opera company to direct something, the usual way in is to be a resident staff producer. This work is generally confined to re-staging revivals, but where directors display exceptional talent, they can be quickly promoted.

The great dissatisfaction about working in opera derives from the pressurized conditions and archaic conventions under which opera productions are rehearsed, especially in the big companies. There were complaints of insufficient rehearsal time and in some cases the non-availability of international stars to rehearse the principal roles.

Kate Brown thought that the most successful directors she knew of - with one or two exceptions - tended to be ''brilliant at creating productions that work like corsets: do up the laces right and it doesn't make much difference who's playing; it will look right, rather effective and anonymous, inside an expressive and probably very handsome concept.''

Opera directors seem to have three options: either to accept that the director's role is merely to 'direct traffic'; to refuse to work under those conditions, which means not working with certain companies or certain singers; or to try and bring about change by pressing for the conditions one finds acceptable.

Both Jonathan Miller and Peter Hall have been able to build up a special relationship with a particular company; respectively, the English National Opera and Glyndebourne. At Glyndebourne, according to Peter Hall, the director is as important as the musical director. He could have four weeks' rehearsal, working on the set from the first day. With the further exception of Bayreuth Festival Theatre, Hall believed that in all other international opera houses, ''the director is an inconvenience.''

What he found difficult to understand was the complete split in opera; that there was an acceptance of both subservient directors, and dictatorial 'concept' directors: ''Many opera productions are a joke,'' said Peter Hall, ''and many opera directors are jokes because they are, most of them, highly intelligent, highly musical people who behave as butlers, who make sure the singers get on the stage and don't bump into each other. On the other hand there's the whole school of subjective opera directors, particularly in Europe; in an age when we're passionate about purity of the text and authenticity, the director is encouraged to betray all the composer's stage directions and all the composer's intentions in order to show his own fantasies, which is a paradox I simply don't understand.''

One of the deepest frustrations for opera directors is the necessity of working with singers who may have the greatest voices in the world, but look completely unsuitable for the roles they are playing and cannot act. Much of the blame was laid on the audiences who accepted this. Peter Hall: ''The public is quite content to see somebody who's 55, as fat as a tank, and can't act, providing they have a good voice. If they want to see them, let them. I don't want to watch them when I can listen to them at home, and I certainly won't direct them.''

Jonathan Miller was equally scathing of the way certain international opera stars work. ''There are dim-wit celebrities who simply, because they've usually done the role many, many times, have a standard version. There are singers who just simply ought to be delivered to the theatre in a van with a slatted ramp and do their thing. They're sacred beasts. They're famous for their singing and they're buggered if they're going to do any smart-arsed idea that you have got as a director. If you have what Coral Browne once described as 'two hundredweight of condemned veal', you don't direct them, you simply transport them.''

Tim Albery emphasized that when international singers perform in revivals they often have no rehearsal at all. Consequently some of them develop a series of what he called ''stock international gestures. As you don't know anyone else you're on the stage with, you can't afford even to look at them because they may not be where you think they're going to be.''

The example was cited of one eminent singer who, because of busy schedules, sent a stand-in to the first three weeks of rehearsals for a new production at Covent Garden, then appeared a few days before the dress rehearsal. Ironically, such practice mirrors the resentment actors expressed about the over-inflated power of directors. At the same time, attitudes are changing because so many major productions are now televised. Here, a different set of values applies. In contrast to the people who fill international opera houses, the television audience is less inclined to accept bad acting or unsuitably cast performers.

9. The Pressure of the Job

"The hardest job I've ever done is directing a play." Peter Hall

Anyone contemplating a career as a director should ask themselves seriously whether they think they could stand the pressure, especially the tension that occurs at the end of rehearsals. In the theatre, a technical rehearsal may be a shambles with everything going wrong, the actors exhausted and disillusioned, and the imminent possibility that the production is not going to work. At an opera dress rehearsal, the conductor may make a sarcastic comment about the singing of an aria causing the leading tenor to walk out. A television director may desperately want to do another take of a scene, but finds that studio time has almost run out and the floor crew will all have to be put on overtime, which would mean going over budget. On location, a film director may have to wait for a technical problem to be fixed while hundreds of bored extras roam all over the set, valuable rehearsal time with the actors is being eaten up and the light is going.

At some point in a production, directors, actors and technicians may find themselves working to the limits of their endurance just to get the show on: there is something about the nature of dramatic performances that makes people go beyond the call of duty. Even rigid union rules cannot entirely cushion people against this. Inevitably, it takes its toll, and many directors, caught up in a spiral of success, have soon found themselves burnt out, grasping for short-cuts and settling for clichés in place of the high ideals they may have set out with. So what role can training play in that?

Peter Hall thought these problems can be prepared for at the training stage; for example, how to pace oneself and keep oneself objective. But he emphasized that there is no getting around the fact that directing is an extremely taxing and stressful job: "I have done in my life, hard academic labour, hard managerial labour and hard physical labour, and I'm bound to say the hardest job I have ever done is directing a play. It's harder than directing a film because from the moment you begin you are working at full stretch to the moment you end. The actors have moments when they're off, but for a director, you are at high tension throughout the rehearsal period. We all know directors who slumber off. But if you're actually doing it, it is the most tiring activity - emotionally and physically - I know."

Worst of all is the climate of fear in which most directors work and the qualities that are needed to survive in it. Some saw this as a kind of sickness. Jamie Nuttgens: "The character of directors is the character of theatre in Britain. The characteristics of our theatre and the bodies that feed it are disunity, secrecy, competitiveness and paranoia. To train a healthy generation of directors, these faults would have to be overcome and the confidence, support and free communication provided to make overt defensiveness unnecessary."

Summary

This Enquiry has taken place against the background of a gathering debate that questions the very role of the director. Is our theatre becoming 'director's theatre'? Are actors right to depose the all-powerful director? Do we really need directors at all?

The complexity of the issues stems from the fact that a director is different things to different people, and the spectrum of ability ranges from genius to incompetence. The complaints against directors are, in many cases, well-founded. Too often there has been an unacceptable standard of behaviour in the way directors have treated the people working with them. The passion of the arguments derives in part from the irony that in any dramatic production, live or recorded, the director, who is the leader, may well be the least trained person involved. It is a maverick role.

In the survey we conducted, the most telling statistic is the one that says 55% of all directors indicated they had no formal training as a director (for theatre directors the figure is 64%). The lack of training opportunities has made directors vulnerable to attack. Their implicit amateur background means that directing has become a job that all-comers can take on: writers are directing, actors are directing, stage managers are directing, even critics are directing.

At the same time there is the deeply serious movement of the auteur director who either writes the script or bends a given text to illustrate a point he/she wants to make. This imposing of a concept can, in the right hands, produce some of the most stimulating theatre and film of our time; in lesser hands it can distort what good directing is all about.

The other facet is what might be called the 'actor's director', a less visible figure who is chiefly concerned to get good, honest performances from actors and to unlock what the writer is trying to say.

Certainly, there are fashions in directing, as there are in acting or design or playwriting. It has been our job on this Enquiry to determine what are the lasting values on which good directing depends and how they might be nurtured.

As the evidence has shown, the director is ideally an extraordinary figure, often embodying all sorts of qualities and contradictions. There is the need for both strong leadership and willing collaboration; the ability to manipulate actors and still to be sensitive with them; the capacity for flair and dashing originality on the one hand, and complete selflessness on the other. Not surprisingly, of the thousands of directors working in Britain, few measure up.

An analogy was frequently made with the conductor of an orchestra, another figure who may have had little formal training but who most likely came to the job through performing music, and will therefore be a highly-trained musician. Pursuing the analogy, the experience of acting seems to be a useful

V

tool to directors, but it is more important to know how to communicate with the actors.

Most of the complaints that we heard revolved around the professional relationships between directors and the people they work with. All too often there is a rift. Its seriousness is evident in the way that many actors felt it was actually dangerous to speak out against directors for fear that they might be labelled as troublemakers, which could affect their employment opportunities.

To a certain extent, power is inherent in the job of directing. There is an indispensable decision-making function. So long as directors are aware of this and use their position in a responsible and sensitive way, the relationships can be productive and harmonious.

There are two sides to the profession: the directors and the directed. A tradition has evolved whereby actors allow directors to have power. But actors can also bring about change, for example by setting up companies where the actors employ the director. Renaissance Theatre Company is one example.

The rift has also been aggravated by the way in which many of the good qualities of directors go unnoticed by critics and public alike, while many of the bad qualities of directors are obscured by good acting and production expertise. All these factors reinforce the 'them and us' attitude which has pervaded the evidence to this Enquiry. Taking the evidence together, it is easy to derive the impression of a strife-torn profession where working relationships are built on ignorance, suspicion and dishonesty. Of course this is by no means universally true. There was evidence of much highly-skilled work and indeed the majority of people we heard from, on both sides, found their work satisfying on the whole, otherwise they would not have remained in the business.

However, the evidence of this Enquiry overwhelmingly supports the view that the training of directors in Britain is grossly inadequate and that the existing provisions for training need urgently to be improved. Under the present conditions, success in directing demands a certain toughness, which helps explain why there has been such a growing friction between directors and the people who work with them. One of the most important things a thorough training for directors could do would be to start to mend the rift and create a more unified sense of talented people working together in a climate of integrity and mutual respect, giving of their best.

We must now examine how that training could be possible.

PART TWO

TRAINING TODAY

Chapter VI

QUESTIONS OF TRAINING

VI

This chapter summarizes the many views we received on whether training is useful and what some of the best solutions for training directors might be. The main issues are as follows:

1. The Necessary Ingredients

In our questionnaire we asked directors to list what they considered to be the ten essential ingredients in a directors' training course. This is what they chose, in order of popularity:

Theatre
* Experience of working with actors
* Ability to evaluate, analyse and edit a text
* Personnel and communication skills
* Ability to judge acting, design, stage management and other technical talent
* Organizational skills and the ability to handle budgets
* Knowledge of movement, speech and voice techniques
* Applied knowledge of acting
* Ability to use improvisation where appropriate
* Wide knowledge of world drama and the history of world theatre
* Knowledge of stage and costume design

Television
* Experience of film/video and sound editing
* Personnel and communication skills
* Ability to evaluate, analyse and edit a text
* Organizational skills and the ability to handle budgets
* Experience of working with actors
* Understanding continuity for film and television
* Ability to judge acting, design, stage management and other technical talent
* Ability to use film and/or TV cameras and sound equipment
* Understanding lighting techniques
* Understanding the use of music in a production

Film
* Experience of working with actors
* Understanding continuity for film and television
* Ability to evaluate, analyse and edit a text
* Personnel and communication skills
* Ability to judge acting, design, stage management and other technical talent
* Organizational skills and the ability to handle budgets
* Ability to use film and/or TV cameras and sound equipment
* Understanding lighting techniques
* Understanding continuity for film
* Ability to research

We also asked directors to name the two types of director training opportunity that would have been most valuable for the work they do now. This was the order of popularity:

Theatre
* Attachments
* Professional course
* Short courses
* Drama school course
* University course
* Polytechnic or HE course

Television
* Attachments
* Professional course
* Short courses
* Drama school course
* University course
* Polytechnic or HE course

Film
* Professional course
* Attachments
* Short courses
* Drama School course
* University course (nil for Polytechnic or HE)

TABLE 11 - MOST VALUABLE TRAINING OPPORTUNITY

KEY

A) Short courses B) Attachments C) University course D) Polytechnic or HE course
E) Drama school course F) Professional course G) Other

It is significant that in all three categories (theatre, film and television) attachments and professional courses are the most sought after, yet sponsored attachments in theatre are now down almost to single figures, whilst professional directing courses are almost non-existent: they are available in film and television schools but entry is extremely competitive. Short courses are also rare and usually limited to members of closed organizations, like the Actors Centre or the Directors Guild.

There are only three drama school courses for directors in the country: The Drama Studio Ealing, East 15 Acting School and the Royal Scottish Academy of Music and Drama. That leaves universities, polytechnics and colleges of higher education. These are reasonably accessible, but they figure lowest in the survey, which suggests that directors already working have little faith in them as a way into the profession.

The following sections discuss some of the elements required in any course that aims to cover all the training needs of a director.

a. Directing Theatre

One of the most widely expressed views was that, before putting theory into practice, trainee directors should be required to see lots of theatre and film. It was pointed out repeatedly that many directors make a habit of not going to see other directors' work, and that on the whole, directors do not see nearly enough theatre. There should also be emphasis on seeing examples of world theatre, possible now with the increasing number of companies visiting Britain through various festivals. As the critic Joyce McMillan pointed out, seeing theatre does not always mean needing to see the best. ''The thing that young directors miss is seeing bad shows - how actors cope with bad direction and bad scripts. They miss the kind of run-of-the-mill experience of seeing all the things that can happen in the theatre.''

In terms of personnel skills, the point was made that the theatre lags behind other professions. As Patrick Malahide said, ''I do think directors ought to be taught group dynamics and people management in a much more systematic way. People who are shy have to cope with a group of actors coming into a rehearsal room in the morning, and if this was industry that would be tackled. Videos ought to be used so that the director, directing a group of people can actually see what his body language is saying.''

Content, of course is paramount. As Joyce McMillan cautioned, the key thing about communication is having something to communicate. ''That's the thing all people with technical skills spot a mile off - when the director is actually just bullshitting.''

A year's stage management was advocated as a good way to see everything that is going on, whilst having a function at the same time. However, adminstrative skills should not be neglected: an understanding of grant applications, employment legislation, wages and national insurance, contracts and quarterly returns are a necessary part of the director's knowledge.

The value of a university background was extolled by Jonathan Miller: ''I feel a deep commitment to the idea that this comes out of a culture and that actually what you know has a bearing on what you do - contrary to what the English think, who feel the more you know the less you can do. I feel that it arms the vision, that's all.''

As for things like space awareness, Miller, like many other directors, had a pragmatic approach that rested on the individual's power of observation. ''I would encourage people to look at the groupings in rooms and how people sit and stand, and different types of crowds, different types of conversation, how people come together. What I am encouraging is the introduction of things into courses which don't figure at all. The aesthetics of compositions will come out of what you have observed. In fact all the rules of the theatre are provisional. They're there to be broken and readjusted.''

b. Directing Opera

Donald McIntyre was a strong advocate of a full-scale training course for opera directors, probably attached to a music college or opera company where there would be access to singers, but where trainee directors could work under the supervision of experienced directors and singing teachers.

One of the problems of letting trainee directors work with opera students in music colleges like Guildhall or the Royal College of Music, is that almost every opera production is seen as a high-profile showcase. It is also still very much a teaching situation. Therefore, care is taken that the most experienced directors are brought in to work with singing students.

Kate Brown, one of the few women opera directors, advocated some sort of workshop situation in which directors, conductors and singers could work together in different ways and with different techniques. She also called for an organization that would run courses and classes in various technical skills, like lighting and design, as well as courses on different ways of approaching a text, or the use of improvisation, dance and mime. "However, an integral part of this organization must be that it is linked to the colleges of music and drama, and to the numbers of small semi-professional companies and opera clubs," she said. "You will only get directors to retrain if you subsequently let them practise their newly honed skills."

c. Directing Dance

Although there is no formal training opportunity for a choreographer to learn how to brief a designer, how to run a technical rehearsal or how to communicate with dancers, the problem has seldom arisen because most choreographer/dance directors have been dancers themselves and therefore have a wealth of practical experience to draw on. It is similar to the situation of a prominent actor becoming a director.

VI

The training that exists, for example the choreographic course at the Royal Ballet School, concentrates almost exclusively on the creation of dances rather than the staging of them. Because the majority of dance works are competently staged, there is not the sense of crisis about director training that exists in the theatre.

However, like theatre directors, dance directors learn by doing it and by gradually eliminating initial mistakes. As David Bintley recalled, "The first ballet I did was 25 minutes long and it had something like 40 lighting cues. Well, you learn fairly quickly, because the next night you go out and a cue is missing, or it's irrelevant."

Also, because of the economic pressure, especially on ballet productions, many young choreographers never get a second chance. It would therefore be useful for choreographic courses to include at some point, the technical aspects of staging a dance production. Many of the issues and recommendations covered throughout this report are therefore relevant to dance.

Lack of facilities is one of the main reasons why the staging of dance is not covered in choreographic courses. However, the Royal Ballet is hoping that the provision of a new studio theatre in the Royal Opera House (as part of the proposed rebuilding programme) will give new choreographers the experience of staging their work in a more relaxed environment.

d. Directing Film and Television

Stage directors have often made an easy transition to opera. Making the transition to film was reckoned to be much harder, not only because of the technical skills involved. As Richard Eyre found, ''Working in theatre is the worst possible training for filming. I think it teaches you everything you have to discard for film-making. It took me a long time to realize that.''

Criticism of film and television training centred on two weaknesses: very little work with actors or on acting problems; and not enough work with writers on the processes of developing a script.

There was also criticism from directors and actors of the television training schemes offered by both BBC and Independent Television companies. Quality in director training was felt to be especially important at this time. As Roy Battersby said, ''With the prospect of an industry dominated by the Murdochs and Maxwells, it is vital that we don't just end up with new generations of whizz-kid directors without a thought in their head. All great directors have something to say.''

2. The Independent Talent v. Institutionalized Training

Most people conceded that the director is a creative artist, just as an actor or a conductor is an artist. At the same time it was almost unanimously accepted that there is a strong element of craft in directing, and that it comprises many teachable skills. How much of the job can be taught will be discussed in the following sections. The majority believed there was a place for a system of training that would give trainee directors many of the necessary skills away from the pressure of public exposure. A minority of directors, who themselves had made very successful careers without formal training, did not see a great need for this.

The negative side of formal training is that, if wrongly handled, it could impose a pattern or mould that might flatten out the individual creative spirit and the capacity for original thinking. Several directors and performers spoke of a stylistic sameness that could arise as it has sometimes done in Eastern Europe where there is a strong history of directorial culture. Almost all British directors agreed that it is crucial to preserve their differences. Any scepticism towards formalized training was based on that view.

There was also widespread agreement that it is almost impossible to find, let alone teach, any kind of formula that will reproduce the intangible and complex qualities of great directors.

3. Is Formal Training Really Necessary?

The people who worked with directors were, on the whole, strongly in favour of there being a level of professional director training that more closely matches the standards of training applied to actors in Britain. However, directors themselves were significantly divided on whether there is a place for formal training at all. What has to be taken into account here is that any admission of the need for a three or four-year professional training for directors implies that one's own background is entirely inadequate. So we were bound to encounter a lot of disguised defensiveness.

Those few who had been through a proper training, usually abroad, were convinced that was the answer. In the absence of this, most people favoured attachments and the assistant director experience, because that was the way they entered the profession. ''Probably the best training is not by 'course' but by working as assistant, however humble, in a practising company,'' said Lindsay Anderson, who had been rejected by both the Bristol Old Vic Theatre School and the BBC Television training course.

But it was widely agreed that attachments to theatres or film companies to observe and assist, as the final stage of training, probably give directors the best possible preparation.

There was also support for some kind of directors' institute to be set up, where even senior and experienced directors could come and do research as a way of recharging themselves. With the increasing emphasis on sabbaticals for artistic directors, this could be an effective way of co-ordinating advanced study opportunities.

VI

Views on the need for formal training varied widely. On the one hand, there were sceptics like Terry Hands, who said, ''I suspect it is a waste of time. If I had to describe a course I would say: (i) Learn a musical instrument (ii) Learn how to paint (iii) Learn a foreign language. Some kind of semi-formal training in psychology would be hugely helpful. I think as far as learning craft and technique are concerned that could be done through the occasional master class.''

On the other hand, there were firm supporters like Oliver Neville, who warned that director training should not be a kind of cosmetic course. It should be integrated with the work of putting on practical professional theatre. ''What worries me are courses which don't dig deep enough into all aspects of directing,'' he said. ''And in this country universities, by and large, are not equipped to provide practical vocational training. Training for directing should be at least as profound as the acting training we're doing here at RADA at the moment. Not to have this training can be very dangerous because the norm is for someone to leave university, become a director, and try their teeth out on a whole lot of experienced actors until they've learnt the job. That used to happen in weekly rep, quite out of the way. But more and more this is happening in very exposed areas quite quickly. It's not exactly a rational way of getting good directors in the theatre.'' This argues against siting a professional training course in a university drama department, but for linking it to a working theatre.

Peter Brook summarized the issues in this way: ''One can't generalize. A director can only work out of his particular talent, personality, experience, attitude to life etc, so each director has to be considered a case apart. At the same time, he can be helped in his formation. In what way? There are two basic paths. The assistant (watching the work of someone more experienced) or the 'do-it-yourself' (learning by one's own mistakes in direct contact with the raw material). Again one path will suit one temperament, one will suit another. Personally, I favour the second way. I think nothing develops more fully than trying and doing.

''For this, the learning director needs a group of actors and an audience. I feel that here he must not be blocked by the illusion that unless he has a well-equipped theatre, a decent budget, and professional actors he can't get going. On the contrary, he must accept that a beginner, happily and healthily, is the lowest common denominator.

''All our work with The Centre [International Centre of Theatre Research] playing improvisations in non-theatrical contexts convinces me that if a director gets together a few people, a would-be writer and borrows a room, and gets together a handful of people, he can start. Then he's like the the the nineteenth century painter with pencil and sketch book at a life-class, or in a café. If he can't beg, borrow, steal and persuade, he'll never have the stamina to go all the way later. If he does, however, he will begin to learn for himself and define in his own way what he wants to do and say.''

4. Can Directing Be Taught?

"You can't train someone to be an artist - you can only give them a technical training." Stewart Laing

There was general agreement that there are skills in directing that can be taught, whether in a three-year course or a weekend workshop. This can produce, at the very least, competence in a director.

But the difference between a great director and a mediocre one depends on a whole range of indirect intangibles which are harder to define or pass on. Perhaps the most basic of these is talent. Without that, all efforts are wasted. In discussing the merits of training, we will assume that a trainee has some talent for directing in the first place. The analogy with actor training is useful. As Flloyd Kennedy explained, ''There is a theory that you can't train an actor. You certainly can't train one to be any good, but it's been proven, I think, that you can give them a technique. You can give them a training which they can bring their own ability to.''

It is also unreasonable to expect too much of training, whatever the profession. The limits and uncertainties of training were considered by Max

Stafford-Clark, who said, "The irony is that the correlation between training and skill is so indirect. You can train directors for years, and never be clear until you push them out of the nest, whether or not they can direct."

As Ken Howard pointed out, "Flair, eye, communication and judgement are not curriculum subjects." The intangibles were likened to the bedside manner of a doctor, not an easy thing to teach. Jonathan Miller's opinion was: "You don't teach it - you just know that some people have got it and some people haven't, which is why I think on the whole that schools of directing are a complete waste of time."

5. Career Structure - Director or Manager?

It is difficult to resist the career structure in the theatre whereby one earns a reputation as a director and is eventually offered the post of artistic director. Those who start up their own company are thrust into this position almost immediately and their managerial skill grows as the company becomes more successful. Arguably, it is a fine training, although many potentially exciting theatre groups continue to collapse through artistic mismanagement.

But for those who have worked for a long time as associate or freelance directors, the sudden gear-change can come as a shock. It inevitably drags them away from the rehearsal room and into the board room. It calls for a whole set of skills for which they may have neither the training nor the aptitude.

VI

Terry Hands on the RSC: "We're a £17 million a year break-even operation, which we normally just make. And none of us have been trained to run a £17 million a year operation. We are at this moment bringing in all kinds of firms to help us organize an industry this big."

Richard Eyre saw the producer's role as an essential part of the artistic director's job. "That's my view of Peter Hall's great talent," he said. "He's a brilliant producer in that he will come into a run-through and tell you what's wrong in a most encouraging way. And what he'll provide you with is only what he knows to be achievable in the time. That's real skill to be able to do that. I think anyone who runs a theatre has got to take on board that producing role. But the only training for that is training by example."

Although our brief was initially to confine ourselves to the training of the director as the person who works on the rehearsal floor, it seems that at a certain stage in a directing career the full range of managerial skills needs to be looked at.

6. Whom Do Trainee Directors Direct?

In film and television schools the problem is solved by hiring professional actors who might otherwise not be working, and by paying them allowances. An Equity agreement covers this, so that, in the event of a film being subsequently sold, the actors are paid an adequate fee. This seems to work to everyone's benefit, since the average engagement might be only four or five days. Theatre training institutions have so far not been able to do this because the rehearsal periods are longer. Even if the actors are paid only expenses, the whole operation becomes extremely costly. The Drama Studio does, however, seem to get around this at times.

The alternative is for trainee directors to direct their peers who may not have any special aptitude for acting. In practice this sometimes results in a great deal of aggression and aggravation, as student directors set about testing their skills in a kind of bear-pit situation. Oliver Neville: "I would not normally put a directing student with acting students. I mean, it's the blind leading the blind." There is no consensus on this issue. Some institutions have claimed that their drama students enjoy working with trainee directors and even do some of their best work with them: we had more evidence of drama students resenting the experience.

Most directors and actors felt that the ideal is to have trainee directors working with experienced professionals. Martin White of Bristol University Drama Department said that the one thing student directors needed was to work with actors who were better at it than they were at directing. "The trouble is that in institutional courses you haven't got that facility. My students who are working out whether they want to become directors are working with people who themselves are working out whether they want to be actors."

7. Attachment and Observer Schemes

A theatre attachment means that a trainee director will spend a certain time - usually up to a year, sometimes two years - in a theatre, doing a variety of jobs at the discretion of the artistic director. Usually the trainee will have some experience in this theatre as an assistant director. It is the nearest thing to an apprenticeship.

The problems with attachments are twofold: very few of them are funded; the quality of the training experience varies enormously, depending on the theatre.

There is a powerful argument for increasing the funding for attachments, as this is still the best way into the profession through practical experience. The vulnerability of attachments is that, if a theatre is paying for its own assistant director and is facing cuts, then this is one of the first jobs to go. However reluctantly, attachments are usually seen as a luxury. Nevertheless, care needs to be taken to ensure that a network of capable directors is used on any attachment scheme. Many trainees have complained either that they learnt all the wrong things, or that they learnt by negative example. Several older directors thought this was not a bad thing.

Observer schemes are also valuable, though over a long period ambitious young directors have voiced their frustration at having no function in the rehearsal room. The main problem with observer schemes is that some of the best directors cannot bear to have anyone watching them while they work - Peter Brook and Trevor Nunn among them. Actors start performing instead of exploring and the director plays directing. However, it must be said that a great many fine directors are not bothered by it, and the Directors Guild Observation Scheme, operating across theatre, film and television, has worked satisfactorily for its members.

In the organization of attachments and observer schemes, consideration should be given to the fact that not only companies belonging to the mainstream of theatre are worth observing. Directors should be encouraged to broaden their knowledge through periods spent with TIE companies, experimental companies, mime companies and so on, as their specialized working methods can provide a valuable learning experience. The opportunity for cross-media observation was also seen as desirable; so that a film director could see a theatre company rehearsing, and a stage director could watch how films are made.

Currently there is no overall co-ordination of attachments, and insufficient monitoring. An independent body to monitor training and to whom trainees could go for information, advice and the resolution of difficulties, is essential. This body should be authorised and prepared to mediate between the trainee and the theatre management in the event of any conflict.

VI

The selection procedure for attachments and bursaries needs more careful consideration. It was in this area that the greatest criticisms arose. There were strong suggestions that actors should be involved on the selection panels, as their instinct is useful in determining the potential of a director. Nor should schemes be confined to, or biased in favour of graduates. The presentation of oneself should not be confused with directing potential. Paul Unwin suggested, "The way it works at the moment is that a specific eloquence gets through, and that doesn't prove you can direct. I think that the theatre accepts bad directors in a most bizarre way."

Christopher Oxford asked, "On what criteria are applicants for the Regional Theatre Young Directors Scheme, the BP Young Directors Scheme, the various bursary schemes and the publicly-supported university courses shortlisted, and why is there an implicit expectation that they will already have had directorial experience? Is there for each course an optimum type of trainee being sought, with a certain track-record, like the 'demonstrable commitment to Scottish theatre' understandably required by the Scottish Arts Council Trainee Directing Bursary? Why does the chief Arts Council of Great Britain scheme rely on a largely redundant game of mass hide-and-seek in search of a willing sponsor company? Why is the only manifest observer's scheme run by the exclusive Directors Guild, when demonstration is the most effective form of directorial teaching possible?

''I ask because I feel that proper opportunities should not hinge on having good contacts, or being in the right place at the right time: too many people are barred from formal training by factors which have nothing to do with their aptitude for directing.''

If there are so few opportunities for trainee directors to get into theatres, then the issue should also be addressed by the theatres themselves, and indirectly, by the organizations that fund them. David Thacker suggested, ''I would make it a condition of subsidies to regional theatres that they employ at least one associate director - preferably three directors on the staff - the artistic director, an associate director and a trainee director.''

8. A Role for Assistant Directors

Where so many attachments come unstuck is that the host theatre does not have the time to train, or does not even have a clear policy about how to use trainees. Artistic directors are often unaware of the potential. Many directors admitted that they do not know what to do with assistants. Some find in them the comfort of a sounding-board, which is not always fulfilling for the assistant.

Terry Hands recalled, ''When I worked as an assistant myself with John Barton, I was carrying pints of milk and 600 mentholated cigarettes. It varies very much on what the initial relationship is. These days [at the RSC] we try to give them something more. The only official on-paper role is rehearsing the understudies, and to maintain the show during its run.''

Max Stafford-Clark thought that it makes sense to have assistants for a long period - ideally two years - because in that time one can give them experience of all departments and functions like script meetings, assisting the front-of-house manager, publicity department and so on. ''But they would specifically assist on a couple of productions. I would never - particularly working in London - guarantee to give a production to an assistant; it's not like the Traverse, or the Liverpool Playhouse where you've got relative privacy.''

Trevor Nunn, on the other hand, could not stomach the term 'apprentice' or the notion of a formally declared relationship of apprenticeship with a younger director. ''What I look for in an assistant is another point of view, a sympathetic intelligence. I would be looking for somebody who would challenge me, question me, provide alternative thinking. Not somebody who would be taking notes on what I am doing.''

In the absence of a formal apprenticeship, one of the great strengths of assistant directorships is that they can provide the most immediate way of passing on skills from one generation of directors to the next. Trevor Nunn owed much to Peter Hall. Mike Leigh, who assisted John Barton, Peter Hall and Trevor Nunn at the RSC, recalled that ''as a 24-year-old, I was able to cut my teeth on a wide range of skills and ideas; these helped me not only to learn how to *approach* directing and staging problems, but also how to *become a director.*''

Peter Gill had a similar experience under George Devine at the Royal Court where he assisted Anthony Page, Lindsay Anderson and William Gaskill. He also acted in some of their productions. ''I was lucky enough to work in a theatre that had a policy of developing talent,'' he recalled. Now Peter Gill has his own programme for developing young directors at the Royal National Theatre Studio (see Chapter VII, 5).

It is interesting at this point to contrast the attitude towards apprentices in the rest of Europe: on the whole they serve a very long apprenticeship, attached to one director for up to five years. This narrows the working experience to the methods of one individual and postpones the moment of the apprentice's first production. So there are not so many young people doing productions. But it does give a deep, if somewhat ponderous, insight. As Clive Barker pointed out, ''Eugenio Barba spent three years watching Jerzy Grotowski before he mounted his first production. That is too long, I'm sure, as he says he was in a total state of panic when the moment came, not knowing how to begin, but what he learned has been the basis of his work with Odin over nearly 25 years.''

David Thacker described his trainee programme at the Young Vic: every production has an observer for all of the rehearsals and there is an assistant director post with a year's contract. ''When interviewing [for an assistant] I look for common ground - the way they talk about plays, the way they talk about acting. I suppose that acting is the centre of my interest as a director.'' Apart from assisting on productions, part of the job is to conduct the theatre's actor auditions which involves interviewing up to 30 people a week and working on their pieces. ''So she gets the experience of working with an actor who comes in with his piece of *Hamlet* or whatever. Maybe she hasn't read *Hamlet*. She has to engage with him and help him through it. This is extremely valuable experience for the trainee and positive for the actor. We get lots of letters from actors thanking us for the fact that that has happened.

''There's no commitment that she will direct a play. When the right time comes, if I believe her to be the right person to direct a play that we are doing, then I will ask her to direct it.''

Assuming that he has an assistant he can trust, Thacker has found that the post is actually cost-effective because it relieves him of a number of duties while giving a trainee director valuable experience. ''That is why I feel so passionately about demanding that theatres do it. There have been so many occasions when people say, 'Oh I can't afford it, can't afford the £9,000 or £10,000.' Yet the development of the theatre in this country is crucially dependent upon the quality of the directors that we have.''

VI

9. Mid-Career Training

"I've forgotten what other directors do in rehearsal because I haven't watched anybody for 10 years." Paul Unwin

Many actors talked about the defensiveness of directors and their suspicion of other people's work. Directors themselves voiced the feelings of isolation and loneliness once they were in the profession. As Jane Lapotaire put it to one group of directors, ''One of the huge differences between actors and directors is that we see many of you at work. You don't see any of each other at work. The actor has a permanent learning experience, but the director only has his or her one way.''

Our contact with established directors indicated that there was a huge demand for more mid-career training opportunities. David Thacker: ''I think it would be wonderful if all of us would be able to enrol for a month somewhere and do a very valuable intensive course in particular areas that we don't feel confident in.''

This might not necessarily be confined solely to direct theatre skills: it could for instance involve attachments outside the theatre. As Richard Gough pointed out, ''There is a danger in theatre that you begin to feel that you're special. But actually what makes a successful foreman of an oil rig, or a successful bank manager or an expedition leader to the North Pole is not that different from a successful technique of leadership in the theatre.''

British directors have persistently been accused of an insular and inward-looking attitude towards theatre, being largely ignorant of the work and methods of international figures. If it could be arranged, directing workshops attended by established British directors would be an attractive proposition to directors like Grotowski, Brook, Barba, Suzuki and Schechner. Richard Gough, who has organized many such courses for actors at the Centre for Performance Research in Cardiff, has begun to look into this idea.

10. Quality Control

"Who is going to teach these courses? Please don't let it be the film academics." Les Blair

Some years ago, following the Gulbenkian report *Going on the Stage*, the National Council for Drama Training set up a system of accreditation for drama schools. One of the effects of this was to concentrate the minds of drama school courses in defining what they were actually trying to teach. It also provided, for the first time, an ongoing standard by which the quality of training could be measured.

There is a strong argument for a system of accreditation of directing courses, both professional and within universities and polytechnics. The accreditation body might be the same, or part of the same organization that would watch over the running of attachment schemes.

The problem with director training, such as it is at present, is that there is no overview and no provision for quality control. The standard of work varies enormously. From the prospective student's point of view, the choice of institution has to be made on the basis of very little information. Prospectuses give only the baldest outline and often fail to clarify the main strengths of a course as opposed to what other institutions are offering.

From within the profession there was considerable scepticism about the worth of the drama departments. As Peter Gill said, "I don't think drama departments, as they are organized at present, are of any use because they reflect the prejudices rather than the enthusiasms of the teachers. I would welcome vocational training, particularly if it was linked to an attachment to a theatre. But you would need brilliant people."

Many directors were convinced that only the very best people should teach trainee directors, and that they should definitely be working professionals, as they are at the National Film and Television School. Because of the employment conditions in universities, drama departments are usually staffed by people who currently have very little contact with the profession. Not only the teaching itself would benefit, but the planning of the curriculum. Consultation with leading professionals on a regular basis would ensure that the course was fulfilling a need, and not providing training in a vacuum.

This is not a simple issue to solve. Because professional directors and actors are usually working, they can seldom make a long-term teaching commitment to a school or university. Continuity therefore suffers.

VI

11. How Long To Train?

Before advocating any system of training, we must first recognize that there will be different needs for different people, depending on where they have come from and what experience they have had. This means that the most useful training will have to be flexible, and the time taken to train will vary from one director to another.

To make a comparison, actors frequently pointed out that they are in a training situation for virtually all their professional lives. Learning comes from the experience of working on different roles, and of working with different actors and directors. They also acknowledged that a three-year course in a drama school does not produce ready-made actors: rather it provides a foundation that equips the actor to complete the training through professional experience.

A radical shift in the attitude towards training directors is now needed. A degree in drama will not make a complete director, nor will an attachment to a theatre, nor a course in a drama school. Even a three-year training combining all these would not make a complete director. So it is dangerous to think a director can be fully-trained in a mere three years. It is going to take a much longer commitment.

Our chapter on training abroad makes it clear that this is recognized on foreign courses. The Polish course is four years, the Russian course, five years. The Carnegie-Mellon course is four years without attachments. And in West Germany, a director may have to expect a five-year apprenticeship.

It is also relevant to compare other professions where expectations are of a significantly longer period of study. An opera singer may spend six years in a conservatoire in Britain, and even then will not expect to be fully fledged and able to step into leading roles. Further training will be obligatory. A musician will spend up to seven years training before entering the profession. Postgraduate research leading to a PhD commonly takes at least five years. A doctor will train for seven years before being registered, but will do up to ten years to become a specialist. Even an actor who has joined a drama school after graduating will be doing six years of full-time study before entering the profession.

Seen in this way, it begins to appear that young directors have been led to expect too much too soon. Impatience has all too often led to incompetence. As a result, years of trial and error are taken up in the profession, undoing initial mistakes and filling gaps. It is of course a highly individual matter: some directors progress rapidly; others are unaware of their faults and will never fill the gaps.

Clearly the present system sustains a climate of amateurishness. If the overall standard of work is to improve, fundamental attitudes towards the training of directors must change.

12. Training Needs in Film and Television

There was both support and criticism of the BBC training scheme for directors, and a great deal of criticism of the inadequacy of director training in the independent sector. Some of the Independent Television companies we heard from had no training programmes at all, others trained directors "when vacancies arise."

Against the background of the government's plans to widen the franchise for television broadcasting companies, the issue of director training becomes crucial because, as many people fear, the likelihood is that independent companies will have neither the funds nor the incentive to train directors.

Robert Love, Controller of Drama for Scottish Television, wrote, "I do indeed anticipate that the future changes in television (the White Paper) will affect in-house training. Frankly, the ITV companies will be looking to reduce the number of in-house directors they employ. In other words, the business will tend to go freelance. Individual companies will simply cease to train people and some thought will have to be given as to how training could be organized on a more centralized basis. Perhaps the National Film and Television School at Beaconsfiool will have a role to play, with greater emphasis on training for television."

Monika Barnes, Training Manager for Thames Television, admitted that "to a great extent we have relied on other organizations to provide training and suitable work experience. There is obviously an anxiety that this pool of talent will reduce as a result of the government's White Paper. When we address the question of training directors at Thames, the two schools of thought are: how can we justify the financial investment in training when we don't know our future? Alternatively, we should train because if someone doesn't do it - who will?"

Central Television expressed concern that their level of training would be likely to decrease as their staff numbers were reduced.

As part of its submission (March 1989) in response to the White Paper, the Independent Television Association emphasized that the ITV companies currently spend some £2.5 million per annum on training, both centrally and within each company: "British television production staff have a deservedly high reputation worldwide, and the industry is proud of its exacting standards. Several hundred new jobs have been created this year by the four Sky and three BSB channels. A great many of them have been filled by staff trained by the BBC or ITV. By next year some nine English-language Astra channels and five DBS channels will be transmitting a total of well over 100,000 hours of television programmes per annum, a massive increase on the 30,000 hours currently transmitted by the four universally-available channels. Even allowing for the fact that a high proportion of the additional 100,000 hours will be repeats of material already broadcast, the sheer scale of this explosive growth will strain the resources of the whole industry. Talents and skills of every type will be in considerable demand, not least in the expanding independent sector."

VI

13. Training Needs in Scotland and Wales

"There is still this feeling that anything that comes up from down South is intrinsically better." James Ross

From Scotland and Wales we detected considerable hostility towards London, and England generally, as the power base of British theatre and television. A closer analysis of the causes behind this supports the idea that director training opportunities should not be based on one model, nor located exclusively in England.

As far as Scotland and Wales are concerned, most of the issues already discussed in this report are equally relevant. But there are a few additional points that need special attention.

a. Consolidating an Identity

It is important to note that in Wales the presence of a Welsh-speaking theatre is very strong. There are 14 Welsh-language theatres in all, with other companies doing work in both English and Welsh. The language factor alone would make it difficult for a director unsympathetic to the Welsh language or bi-lingualism to win the acceptance and confidence of the theatre profession in Wales. Indeed, there had been considerable resistance to the importation of what was called 'sub-English' models of theatre by English directors who had an eye on West End transfers.

Although there is not a difference of language in the Scottish theatre, there exists at present a strong interest in developing a more Scottish identity that will release it from what is seen as the dominance of English culture. The feeling, especially among actors, was that this must come from within. Clearly, a great part of the initiative will depend on writers, but it was pointed out that the degree of physical awareness many fine Scottish actors have could be exploited much more in a theatre that relies less on the literary bias of most English drama.

According to Kate McCall, ''The whole artistic feeling in Scotland is only just coming round to the fact, I'm as good as you are. You've only got to go and see the awe with which the English actor is treated in BBC Glasgow.''

b. English Directors

In Scotland, 11 out of 14 theatres are run by English-born directors, although it was pointed out that some of these people were highly committed to Scotland. Nevertheless, the significant number of theatre people who have come north of the border and found work has bred resentment among the profession in Scotland. The situation is exacerbated by the low employment levels in parts of the country.

The critic, Joyce McMillan, thought the English dominance was to do with the literariness of the Anglo-Saxon theatre tradition. ''I assure you that very articulate Scots can still be very easily brow-beaten by people with very confident Oxbridge accents and Oxbridge backgrounds who come into this country. It's not just that they know more about it; often they don't. It's that they have the actual cultural confidence of belonging, as they feel it's the same culture as Shakespeare and everyone. One way to break that is to introduce elements in theatrical training which are less literary, which place as much emphasis on movement skills, on voice, on fight arranging and the physical element of staging.''

These attitudes are reinforced in the television industry, which encourages English directors to work in Scotland by paying them a subsistence allowance. Scottish directors travelling to England, on the other hand, receive no such allowance.

In Wales, English directors do not seem to dominate the theatre so much, partly because of the vigorous commitment to developing a specifically Welsh approach that is free of English ideas. This has tended to exclude outsiders, so that companies like Theatr Clwyd, run by an Englishman, are not typical.

However, the presence of English directors running some of the main repertory theatres in Wales has helped make the mainstream more inaccessible for alternative theatre directors. As Geoff Moore explained, in many ways the theatre feels as if it is going backwards: ''A lot of that alternative work which should now in fact be moving into the circle of mainstream could be ghettoized, and the other area - hack work with three weeks' rehearsal - will simply triumph within a Thatcher economy.''

c. Training for an Indigenous Theatre

If the professions in Scotland and Wales are to evolve an indigenous theatre, then it follows that they will each have their own special training needs when it comes to nurturing a new wave of directors. An English model for training might have a limited use as a starting point, but as soon as possible a more relevant set of priorities should take precedence.

For instance, working with local writers would almost certainly be a very important part of any director training. But a thorough understanding of devised work and some of the techniques of 'physical theatre' might also be essential ingredients. This is an issue that needs more research and consultation within the Scottish and Welsh communities, as it falls outside the scope of this Enquiry.

Scots saw as the potential strength of their position that directors could be trained to think European rather than English. A parallel view was put forward independently in Wales, that the new Welsh theatre might be more international in its outlook and less verbal. Such a view must be partly influenced by the very active training work that has been conducted by the Centre for Performance Research (formerly Cardiff Laboratory). This has meant that over the past decade Welsh directors and actors have had much more chance of coming into direct contact with people like Jerzy Grotowski, Eugenio Barba and Richard Schechner, or with Peking Opera performers and Balinese dancers, than their English counterparts.

VI

The way forward, therefore, is to absorb international influences and to think in terms of a total theatre that is not so dominated by a literary tradition, as the English theatre is seen to be. For this reason, any English-based director training course would be entirely inadequate to meet the needs of Welsh theatre. Well-funded provisions for director training are needed in both Scotland and Wales to service the specific needs of directors working there.

Film and television are subject to the same pressures of nationalist identity and these factors should also be allowed for in any director training schemes. If it is important that English television directors are not seen to dominate, then perhaps more consideration should be given to promotion within the Scottish and Welsh television industries so that people already working in other areas of television can have access to in-service director training should they wish to make the change.

14. Training Needs in a Multi-Cultural Society

"Eventually there will be a change of perception by Brits of what constitutes their culture." Teddy Kiendl

Two main issues are involved here. There are particular training needs for directors who wish to develop a theatre based on Asian, African or Caribbean cultures. At the same time there is the challenging view that all British directors should be trained for a theatre that reflects the rich diversity of cultures existing in this country.

a. Working in a Non-European Theatre

A growing number of directors working in Britain today are concerned with non-European theatre traditions. Although the milieu of their work may be African, Asian or Caribbean, they usually take these cultures as a starting point for some kind of synthesis, rather than transplanting an authentic form from one society to another. Some of these directors have talked of the vital need to gain a full understanding of the culture they are drawing on, so that the result is not merely a superficial ethnicisation.

This highlights specific training needs for directors. For instance, if one is to avoid crude stereotypes, it is necessary to understand that within the Caribbean culture there are many variants. As Yvonne Brewster noted, "Directors pay great attention to getting the right Welsh or Cornish accent, but if you're black, they presume that you can do a West Indian accent. And 90% of the black actors in this country cannot. A directing course should be able to identify these needs and help students recognize the differences."

Directors also need to understand the dances and music of a particular culture and how these can be used in theatre. Any director drawing on Indian traditional theatre will need to understand its acting processes, which often seem to contradict the western approach to acting. As Jatinder Verma explained, "It requires performers to think from the outside in. The dimension of the vessel - the outer form - is known. The role of the individual actor is to fill it. But British actors will sometimes say, 'Are you asking me to eschew naturalism or the interior life of the character?'"

There will also need to be an appreciation that most non-western theatre cultures evolved from oral, not literary traditions, and are therefore more likely to integrate music, dance, song and mime. So the demands they make on a director are quite different from those of a western play. Teddy Kiendl pointed out that "the integration of art forms has only begun to be explored. A lot of the black work here has been an attempt to fit in with the European literary style."

Directors tended to agree that these aspects are best learnt either by seeing a particular form of theatre in its country of origin or by importing experts who are striving towards syntheses of their own in African, Asian and Caribbean countries.

b. Towards a Multi-Cultural Theatre

Once it is accepted that Britain is not an exclusively Anglo-Saxon society, then it follows that the theatre of tomorrow should increasingly concern itself with cultural synthesis. This goes much further than directors casting a few black actors in a Shakespeare production. It means that new pieces of theatre can draw on both European and non-European traditions as a means of portraying contemporary British society.

As Yvonne Brewster emphasized, "It's gone beyond being given an equal voice, or being disadvantaged. It should just be an integral part of any course, so that this fine distinction between black theatre and white theatre will go. Besides, African theatre that's done in this country is not recognized by the Africans as African theatre, because it's done by British people."

There are, of course, a number of instances where the synthesis is already happening. On leaving Britain, Peter Brook chose to work with an international group of actors, exploring the common ground between their cultures to find a universal theatre language. On a smaller scale, John Martin has been doing similar work with Pan Project. And from a specifically Indian starting point, Jatinder Verma has set out to create an international theatre language with his group, Tara Arts. Meanwhile, in Denmark, important work has been done by Eugenio Barba on the meeting points between different theatre cultures.

The significance of all this work is that it offers a stimulating alternative to the literary tradition of realism which has dominated British theatre for so long. But it is crucial that sufficient time be given to the study of forms and traditions in order to know how to use them wisely. Jatinder Verma warned against any tendency to simply lift interesting movements or sequences and put them into a modern play: "That is not confronting different ways of doing theatre - it is simply giving an ethnic colour to your production."

VI

The training of a new generation of directors needs to acknowledge these factors by giving serious attention to non-European theatre traditions. For this reason valuable training opportunities like the London International Workshop Festival and the initiatives of the Centre for Performance Research in Cardiff should increasingly be targeted at directors and not just performers. It is, after all, still directors who change the theatre, not actors.

Summary

The vast majority of directors we heard from conceded that there are identifiable skills in directing that can be taught. Those who were sceptical about formal training were perhaps resisting the implication that their own untrained skills were in some ways inadequate.

However, there is a lot that one cannot teach, and success in directing will depend on a whole range of intangible qualities. Training will not produce a talent that was not there to start with. At the same time, if there is to be training for directors, it should operate on a serious level and it should be set up in a way that will encourage diversity rather than standardization.

As part of their training, directors should work with capable actors, and at some stage they should be able to direct experienced professionals. The understanding of the acting process is a vital element of director training, rated highly by directors in all media. As will be seen in the next chapter, it is neglected on most training courses, especially in film and television.

Although training should be practical, the academic background should not be underrated. There is also a need to see plenty of theatre of all kinds, and directors at all levels should be encouraged to see more of each other's work.

From theatre directors there is a huge demand for attachments, and a complaint that there are so few attachment opportunities. Part of the problem is that not many theatres are capable of hosting a worthwhile attachment because of financial limitations, or the poor standard of resident directors, or because they are unsure of what to do with a trainee. Therefore, the role of the assistant director needs more thought so that it can provide the optimum learning experience. Attachments need not be confined to regional repertory theatres but could include smaller-scale touring companies, provided the standard of work is sufficiently high. Consideration should also be given to the selection procedures on attachment schemes to ensure that they provide equal opportunities.

A radical shift of attitude towards director training is needed. Directors cannot expect to emerge fully-trained from a three-year course at the age of 21; it will take longer. At the same time, training should be seen as a continuing element in a director's career.

As most working directors are not properly trained, the area of mid-career training needs to be opened up because there is a great demand here. Short courses on specific aspects of directing require consideration.

Opera needs to provide a better range of training opportunities for directors through workshops and short courses instead of relying on the present staff-director system, or taking people who are established theatre directors.

Television training for directors is now in jeopardy because of plans to widen the franchise on Independent Television companies. The profession should be vigilant to safeguard the provisions for training under the new system.

The specialized training needs in Scotland and Wales should be looked at separately, and care should be taken about using any model tailored to English needs. In a wider sense, director training should recognize that Britain is now a multi-cultural society and that it is relevant for the theatre to draw on non-European traditions as an alternative to the Anglo-Saxon literary tradition.

A fundamental reason for the paucity of training opportunities and the unsatisfactory quality of many courses is that there is at present no overview and no means of assessing the quality of training. An independent body to fulfil this function is badly needed.

Chapter VII

THE TRAINING THAT EXISTS

VII

1. Universities and Polytechnics

The training of directors cannot really be seen in isolation from the universities and polytechnics. They may not provide the whole answer but they can offer a vital component in a director's training. We detected, on the part of students, considerable misunderstanding and confusion about what a university or polytechnic can give. We also noted that with tighter co-ordination and more liaison with the profession the training could be much more effective.

The courses offered by the drama departments of universities and polytechnics are usually BA Theatre Studies or BA Drama. A number of them extend to postgraduate level. Most class themselves as non-vocational, though a few courses (including those at Hull, Kent and Middlesex Polytechnic) are described as vocational. All are fairly wide ranging and they offer, usually towards the end of the course, the chance for a certain degree of specialization. Most of the academic staff are full-time. Some of them will direct productions and they will usually have had some professional experience in the theatre. Most of them will have since severed those contacts. A few courses will bring in professionals for isolated classes, but this is exceptional. The balance of theoretical and practical work varies widely from course to course.

Before discussing undergraduate courses, it is essential to consider them in terms of their intentions. As they are academic institutions they do not pretend to give a professional training to directors. As they are preparing students for a degree, directing will be one small part of that degree, sometimes one-sixth. Prospective students should be clear about this when they apply, so that they are not disappointed.

a. The Strengths

What then can drama departments give to would-be directors? Their strength is that they can equip students with a thorough knowledge of the history, theory and criticism of theatre and dramatic literature, together with the theoretical background to directing. A cultural context of this sort is of great value to directors because, among other things, it gives them the vocabulary for researching and analysing a text. It may also equip directors with a range of conceptual approaches to a play, though the application of this is widely disputed in British theatre, if not elsewhere in Europe. In many institutions students have the opportunity through production work to gain familiarity with a range of practical skills such as stage management, sound, lighting, set-construction and costume-making.

A good example of how rich these courses can be is the University of Kent in Canterbury. With the directing element headed by Alan Pearlman (an American who worked as associate director of The Open Space with Charles Marowitz), it is a four-year course with the final year being almost entirely practical.

The first year is an interdisciplinary course which can include Psychology, Sociology and Philosophy. Single honours students study post-war British theatre in performance and/or Brecht. There are plans to make this year more practical with an intensive course on stage technology and some performance work.

In their second year students study theatre technology and the history of theatre. They will also either act or do technical work in the productions directed by fourth year students.

The third year includes a study of modern European drama (embracing, for instance, Grotowski and Artaud), and optional courses on stage design, playwriting, women in theatre and theatre funding.

The fourth year has a full-time directing option allowing each student to direct two productions. In their first term they will do workshops on different directorial approaches, focusing on Brecht, Stanislavsky, Boal, Meyerhold, Grotowski and Brook. There will also be workshops on directing problems and on working with actors. The students will direct a short scene (using each other as actors) without costumes, lights or scenery. Additionally, they will begin preparing a pre-production workbook on the play they have chosen to direct the following term, as well as doing an extended research project on a particular director or directorial method.

The second term is centred on their studio production, a one-act play about 40 minutes long, which will have five to six weeks' rehearsal with a minimum of five hours a day. For this they can work with a designer and they have a production budget of around £70, plus a share of the box office takings. Alan Pearlman will sit in on at least five rehearsals of each play; he will offer notes to the director and will give a critique afterwards when the students analyse each other's work. In between rehearsals there will be more workshops on directing problems, and on the taking and giving of notes.

In the final term each student does a full-scale production in the main theatre (the Gulbenkian Theatre, a well-equipped arena space seating about 350 people). They can work with a designer, operating on a budget of £100 plus a share of the box office takings. This is assessed by staff in conjunction with an external examiner.

b. The Limitations

The shortcoming of a drama department is that in a three or four-year degree course (particularly if Joint Honours with another subject) it is not possible to pursue the teaching of directing to any real depth.

The standard of acting in university or polytechnic productions is likely to be lower than that of the average drama school, if only because the amount of practical acting tuition will be far less. This means that trainee directors will often be directing actors of limited ability. Also, one must consider the context of the work from the students' point of view. As one student commented, ''It's a tremendous amount of work to put in for a small part of a degree.''

VII

The department must also allow that the choice of student is limited to those who have a certain number of A-levels and can afford the financial commitment of three or four years study with no guarantee of a job at the end of it. Statistically, this tends to favour white, privileged British students. It also means that would-be directors of exciting talent who may be less strong academically will have to look elsewhere for their training.

Another problem we noted was staffing. As so many directors emphasized, director training needs very close supervision. Under the present university structure, this kind of scrutiny cannot be afforded, and the commitment of some staff is no doubt stretched to the limit. Many courses rely on weekends and the vacations for some of the more intensive directing opportunities, whilst evening work throughout term-time is the norm. Several course directors felt that they would be able to come to grips with the subject only with a further year postgraduate work. But that would involve a total of at least four years of study.

Consequently, students are often directing productions as part of their course work without adequate supervision or consultation. We even heard of cases where students had been operating lights and electrics without a staff technician to instruct or supervise. Student comments supported this: "No staff member came to sit in on rehearsals to see how it was going," "After my production, there was no feedback from anyone. R was the only staff member who came," "You feel you're dragging them away from something that's more important."

Because the priorities understandably tend to be academic, many of the more practical skills of directing will probably be neglected or skimmed over. It was significant that when we questioned students about their knowledge of handling stage space, using improvisation, or understanding the voice and body, they usually admitted ignorance and said that these areas were not really covered.

c. Expectations and Reality

What the students will be looking for from the department is a chance to develop their interest in theatre and to discover what talent, if any, they might have. They will be doing this in the atmosphere of an academic institution operating in some cases with limited theatrical resources.

As Professor Peter Thomson, Chairman of the Standing Committee of University Drama Departments (SCUDD), wrote:

"There may be examples of departments which would teach 'Directing' more determinedly if their facilities were better: but I do not know of them. We have to recognize the problems:

i) of teaching a subject which sounds 'vocational', but which has no career track;

ii) of teaching, as a subject, a skill whose dominance in the English-speaking theatre has more or less coincided with the decline and fall of the English-speaking theatre. Ought the 'laboratories' of university drama departments to be teaching 'alternatives to the director'?''

Although all drama departments cover broadly similar areas of theatre, the manner in which the subject is taught, the emphasis, the degree of practical work and the facilities available vary considerably. These are elements not easily discerned from every prospectus. It is therefore helpful for the prospective student to have detailed information on the courses available in advance of applying. In the absence of this, many students rely on word of mouth.

There is perhaps a need for an impartial publication describing the various courses, setting out the differences and indicating the particular strengths of each drama department. For example, Middlesex Polytechnic has a good reputation for its mask work, Dartington College is noted for its devised theatre and Bristol University has excellent film and television courses.

d. Contact with the Profession

In most university cities there is a local repertory theatre, or at least a significant amount of theatre activity. An exception would be Dartington, set in the countryside near the town of Totnes. In a few cases there is close contact between the university and the theatre. Bristol University, for example, from time to time sets up workshops conducted by actors, directors or designers from the Bristol Old Vic company. Another example is the TIE component taken by postgraduate students at Leeds University. For this practical project the teaching is partly done by the Leeds Playhouse Theatre-in-Education Company.

But in most cases we found surprisingly scant evidence of contact with local theatres. Peter Thomson identified two problems here:

VII

''i) Both theatres and drama departments operate on a pressure-of-time system, and it often has the effect of restricting co-operation despite good intentions on both sides.

ii) There is some mutual mistrust (or misunderstanding?). Drama departments might suspect professional theatres of overvaluing 'mere' product: professional theatres continue to have problems in concentrating on anything outside their own immediate sphere.''

Obvious though it may sound, this is a relationship that could be strengthened as a matter of policy in such a way that it could benefit both sides. The problem lies in changing attitudes.

e. Entering the Profession

When we asked drama department staff what advice they were able to give departing students about further training, or about entering the profession, we found little awareness of the attachment schemes and bursaries available to students. A more organized system of disseminating this information to universities, polytechnics and other training institutions would be helpful.

Drama departments often encourage their students to create their own opportunities, and indeed this has given rise to theatre groups that have stayed together on a professional basis. One obvious example would be Trestle Theatre which originally grew out of work at Middlesex Polytechnic.

The University of Kent actively encourages these initiatives. In the past it has made use of the Manpower Services Scheme to help with finance and is at present hoping to use the new Enterprise Initiative Scheme. It also brings in people from Independent Theatre Council (ITC), Society for West End Theatre (SWET), Arts Council and Regional Arts Associations (RAA) to give students advice on the administrative and funding aspects of running a theatre company. Again, this is exceptional: the ITC has indicated that it would be delighted to go into all universities, but had been asked only by Kent.

The potential of the drama departments as a way into the profession is illustrated by Bristol University which, despite its non-vocational status, could identify at least six former students who have become professional directors since 1981.

f. Opportunity and Initiative

Most students who are interested in directing will have a chance to direct a short scene or a one-act play at some time. But the drama department cannot always guarantee everyone the chance to direct a full-scale play. In fact we met several interested students who had missed out on directing anything at all: reasons given were that there was not enough time, there were difficulties in getting a theatre space, or there were not enough actors available. Hence, apart from workshops, the bulk of the teaching relating to directing will be dealt with on a theoretical level.

For instance, a widely-used exercise is for students to write a commentary on one scene in a play, describing in detail how they would direct it. But recalling the views of directors we spoke to, this would seem to go against all good practice in directing. The best directors, Brook and Hall among them, may have begun like that, but they soon discarded this approach, preferring to be open to what the actors have to offer rather than coming in with a fixed concept.

Arguably, this theoretical preparation could at least give students an informed background from which to improvise when they did finally direct a play. But the experience of professional actors who have worked with young graduate directors does not support this. Furthermore, when this preparatory exercise was put into practice, students described the conflict that sometimes resulted when they tried to impose their concept on their unwilling student cast.

As directors emphasized repeatedly, you learn by doing it, and the fastest way is to do lots and lots of productions. The drama department simply cannot give its students these opportunities within the course time available. This also begins to explain why Oxford and Cambridge in their heyday, even without drama departments, had the edge on all the others. Through an active drama club (or several in the case of Cambridge), the most motivated students could take things into their own hands and make their own opportunities. Indications are that in the days of Trevor Nunn and Richard Eyre there were keen power struggles within the clubs as students vied to drum up their casts and get their productions on. The obstacles only sharpened their drive and made them all the more determined. That is one reason why most of the senior directors we heard from favoured making it as hard as possible for young directors, because they would need all their clout and cunning in the profession if they were to survive. That sense of initiative and determination has emerged as one of the most important qualities in a director.

By contrast, our experience of talking with undergraduates was that, with alarming regularity, they lacked drive, they lacked a clear sense of what they wanted to do, they lacked any sense of reality of what the theatre world was about, and they had none of the naked ambition that you might see in actors auditioning for a drama school. In the security of their drama department, many of them saw themselves as victims rather than changers of the world. Had it all been too easy for them?

Even more disturbing was the fact that many undergraduates we spoke with had seen very little theatre at all. This was through lack of funds, or due to the geographical location or simply from a lack of motivation. Significantly, this tendency was less evident on the vocational courses run by film and television schools, where there was a higher overall level of enthusiasm and a greater sense of going for a goal. The issue is important because one thing shared by almost all successful directors is an appetite for seeing lots of plays and films of all kinds. Many directors counted this as being as important as anything else in their training.

The majority of the students to whom we spoke had complaints about the course they were doing, but they had no solutions on how to improve their lot. Comments like ''We tend to get very cotton woolled here,'' ''I've no conception of a professional director's life,'' ''I came here under a false impression, thinking it would be more practical than it is,'' ''I didn't know what I wanted to do when I came here, and I still don't really. I often think I'd like to work in the theatre,'' were depressingly typical.

VII

Those few who were a little clearer about what they wanted from the course were merely frustrated by the lack of commitment from the others. ''The directing weekend is frustrating because you've only got a handful of people who are vaguely interested,'' said one student about one of the main directing opportunities on her whole course.

Alan Pearlman of Kent University questioned whether students in the drama departments were really too young because they were being taken on ''before any of their career desires and energies have been shaped.'' He was also aware that the current depressed state of the arts, emphasized in the media, had its effect. He found his students over the past few years ''more demoralized and less enthusiastic about the possibilities that are open to them.''

The stimulus that students provide for each other is, as the Cambridge example has shown, extremely important. Julia Bardsley found the formal training at Middlesex Polytechnic "quite poor", but benefited enormously from the facilities and the company she was with. "They encourage you to create your own work, so you have to make your own opportunities, which is very useful in terms of going to the outside world. New work was going on all the time. My year was highly motivated. I was involved in a very exciting year who wouldn't take no for an answer and who were very keen to make their own pieces. The skills came from trying it and doing it." Unfortunately, this example seems to be exceptional.

g. Film and Television

A few drama departments run a joint-degree in Film and Television. Glasgow University does this, Leeds and Sheffield do on their postgraduate course. One of the most respected Film and Television courses, at Bristol University, is described later in this chapter in section 6.

h. Future Funding

The proposed changes in the grant system for universities, whereby students will pay back a loan from the government, are bound to affect future student intakes. For example, if the employment opportunities in the arts are seen to be dismal, then there may be less incentive to study theatre, knowing that it may be very difficult to pay back the loan. As Peter Thomson commented, "It is too early to say what will be the effects of this damn-fool government's attempt to restrict education to the financially confident. If they go ahead, there will certainly be changes in the range of applicants, though I expect that the intelligent operation of admissions officers will limit the effect on the composition of actual undergraduate groups. The government will be able to publish some statistics that prove that everyone has benefited - but you and I (and everyone else) will know how many people have been educationally disenfranchised."

In conclusion, it is unfair to expect university drama departments on their limited resources to carry the weight of professional training. In a way it is right that the courses should be so open, because, built into them should be the likelihood that most students will not necessarily want to become directors.

As exit-profiles show, more students go on to make rewarding careers in other areas of the theatre or the arts generally, than those who become directors. The same thing happens in drama schools: they train actors, but they also produce directors, agents, administrators and playwrights. However, directors are beginning to come through from drama departments; Tim Albery, Julia Bardsley, Paul Unwin and Clare Venables among them.

Where university courses could benefit is from more direct contact with the profession, or even with professional training institutions, so that there could be shared resources. This would give students who do want to become professional directors the best of both worlds.

2. Drama Schools

A drama school cannot normally cover the theoretical ground that a university or polytechnic might, because its priority must be practical work. Its great advantage is that it can offer directing students a deep insight into the acting process by allowing them to work alongside actors as they go through their own training. Furthermore, most drama schools will also be running stage management courses, which provide another valuable facility. For these reasons many people have felt that the drama school is an important environment in which at least part of the training of a director should take place.

One of the most contentious issues in the whole question of training is: whom do student directors direct? In cases where they have directed drama students, this has provoked both resentment and enthusiasm. The ideal would be at some stage to hire professional actors. However, no scheme has been able to afford this.

a. Past Training

To put the drama school courses operating today in context, it will be useful to begin with a brief description of two past courses.

i. The Old Vic Theatre School

One of the most influential drama schools to operate a directing course was the Old Vic Theatre School (1947 - 1952) set up by the French director, Michel Saint-Denis. Its teachers included Glen Byam Shaw and George Devine. Saint-Denis did not see directing as something that grew out of the acting course. Instead, his 'production' students and designers did a one-year stage management course with talks and classes focusing on the stage, scenery, properties, lighting and the preparation of ground plans. There was also a course called 'The Imaginative Background', which was for both production and acting students. This lecture course covered the development of acting spaces, the history of drama, costume and social behaviour of important theatrical periods, with pictorial documentation as a means of research.

At the end of that year, potential directors were invited to stay on for a second year of advanced tutorial work. Christopher Morahan, who attended this, described the course: "We would work very closely with Michel in tutorials, discussing texts, preparing models, taking on Act One of *The Cherry Orchard* and trying to find out about it, or the whole of the play, working as assistant directors in amongst the second-year acting students. And we would do a production of our own during that second year. So at the end of that two years I had not only some sense of the task ahead of me - because there seemed to be so much to learn still - but also a certain amount of qualification."

Although there were restricted opportunities to direct, when students did stage a scene from a play they would work with the acting students.

VII

117

ii. The Drama Centre

A more recent attempt at teaching directing in a drama school was at the Drama Centre. Under the principal, Christopher Fettes, its course existed from 1974 to 1981. It began as a two-year programme, then was expanded to three. There was an average of eight students each year.

The course had two main strands. The first was understanding how the actor functions, and learning to have a technical language to share with actors. The second was the understanding of cultures, texts and the analysis of those texts.

The course was based on three main approaches: the Stanislavsky system (as taught in New York by Uta Hagen and Herbert Berghof); the work of Michel Saint-Denis (as developed in his later school in Strasbourg); and the theory of Movement Psychology derived from the work of Rudolf Laban.

Directing students observed many of the acting classes as well as having their own acting classes. They also took part in rehearsal projects with the acting students. In their second year they began to direct short scenes, and in the third year they would direct one-act plays, at first without sets and costumes, then later with full production. In all these exercises they would direct acting students from the school. Additionally, they would work as assistants to professional directors doing full productions at the school, and they would also have classes on stage design and the history of theatre architecture.

Most of the directing students were foreign because British students failed to get the grants or funding. The course closed because of lack of time, space and money. With very limited rehearsal space, it became increasingly difficult to schedule rehearsals fairly or adequately. Also, as the directors were using the acting students for their projects, it meant that the actors were having their energies and focuses stretched more than was reasonable for their own development. However, according to Christopher Fettes, the actors were very enthusiastic about working with the directing students. He also emphasized that it was healthy and enriching to have directors training alongside actors, especially foreign students who exposed the actors to other cultures, ideas and possibilities.

A two-year directors' course was also set up by Hugh Cruttwell at RADA in 1967. However, this was abandoned after two years, partly because it seemed unfair for acting students to be directed by directing students. However, the present principal, Oliver Neville, has indicated that he is thinking seriously of reintroducing a director training course at RADA.

b. Current Training

Very few comparable courses operate today. We visited three of them: the Royal Scottish Academy of Music and Drama, the Drama Studio, London, and the Bristol Old Vic Theatre School. Each of them has a different approach and aim. East 15 Acting School also runs a directing course.

i. Royal Scottish Academy

The Royal Scottish Academy offers a BA Dramatic Studies with an annual intake of 20 people, two or three of whom may choose to specialize in directing which runs separately from the professional acting course. Its aim is for the students to complete a three-year academic degree in a very practical environment.

The first year consists of lectures, voice and movement classes and scene work. In the second year, all students direct a one-act play, as well as helping with the lighting and stage management on each other's productions. There are places for three students to specialize in directing in the third year. They will assist a staff director on a main production, they will be seconded to a professional theatre, and they will direct a one-act play at the Academy.

ii. The Drama Studio, London

The one-year directors' course at the Drama Studio in Ealing operates as a further training module for students who have already graduated from a university or polytechnic. It offers no degree and does not make graduate status a condition of entry. However, because of the assumption that students will already have covered the academic aspects of directing, like history of theatre, social history or text analysis, the emphasis is almost entirely practical.

Selection procedure
* Candidates audition with the actors, having prepared a set speech.
* They also conduct and lead some improvisations with acting students.
* They prepare a set play and have a one-hour discussion about it with staff.
* There are never more than 4 applicants per day.

Peter Kenvyn: ''In the final and dreadful analysis, it's whether I like them or not.''

VII

Under the supervision of Peter Kenvyn, the course is based on a belief that the director's skills are derived from the needs of actors, so directors begin on the acting programme alongside acting students. The intake (chosen by audition and interview from 50-60 applicants) is between five and seven.

Although the course is not without its problems, its structure and the range of work covered provide a useful model for professional training:

''Term One
* Acting classes. Technical and stage management classes.
* Practical work on picturization and blocking (2x3hr sessions).
* Assisting course directors on actors' productions. Directing each other in short scenes, (evenings).
* 'Non-verbals': asked to use the facilities of the studio - lights, sound and actors (non-speaking) - to create 2 minutes of atmosphere, to see what they come up with.

* Rehearsing actors (drama students) in a 20 minute scene with sound, lights etc.
* Observing a weekend 'get-in' in an outer London theatre.
* Written work continues throughout.
* Weekend seminar (each term) with a visiting director eg Mike Leigh, Deborah Warner.

Term Two

* The emphasis is more theoretical.
* Writing an adaptation and rehearsing this with drama students. Critique by an established playwright.
* Acting class work and rehearsal attendance becomes optional. In this term, trainee directors stop working with acting students.
* 2-week Shakespeare workshop.
* 8x3hr seminars on 'Style'. The 'One-hour': they mount a production, casting from outside the school (professional out of work actors working for nothing). Budget £100-£120. Rehearsals are supervised by a tutor.
* An aim, over the Easter break, to second all directing students to outside theatres as observers. Not always possible because of the limited number of directors who will take observers.
* Further work on improvisation etc.

Term Three

* Visits from Equity, ITC, designers etc. Taught about schemes like BP, RTYDS etc.
* 4x3hr seminars on casting and standard theatre practice.
* Throughout the term rehearse a full-length play, supervised by a tutor and mounted in house, either with students or professional actors. Students responsible for casting.
* 'Outsiders': rehearse a one-act play (part of a double bill) with the acting students after they (acting students) have graduated, or with outside actors if they wish. 2 weeks full-time rehearsal for presentation in an outside theatre. Budget and venue provided. Peter Kenvyn sits in on rehearsals and acts as production manager.''

Ideally, Peter Kenvyn would like to see it as a more co-ordinated three-year course comprising one year in an academic institution, one year at the Drama Studio and a third year on attachment to a theatre. There are plans to expand the building, which would allow more rehearsal and performance space. But financially the course falls between two stools. It has to rely totally on fees because it is not a member of the Conference of Drama Schools (which does not recognize one-year courses) and it is not recognized by the Department of Education and Science (DES) because it is not a degree course. This suggests that educational funding policies should be rethought to allow for the special needs of director training courses.

Past and present students we spoke to were very supportive of the course. What they felt it needed were better facilities (there is only a tiny studio theatre), more guidance about the practicalities of starting their own companies, and more chance for discussion with host directors when the students were on secondment to a theatre.

iii. Bristol Old Vic Theatre School

The Bristol Old Vic Theatre School does not run a course for directors so much as provide an environment where people can learn the necessary skills. Under the direction of Chris Denys, it is mainly for people with a professional background who are mature, motivated, and have a very clear idea of what they are looking for. People coming directly from university and polytechnic drama departments have in the past been discouraged because it is felt they cannot provide their own incentives, and when they are attached to theatres, "they tend to vanish into the woodwork." There are places for up to four directors.

For the first three weeks the directing students join the acting students in formal classes. The attachments are for 34 weeks and can be arranged anywhere the trainee wants. At the same time, trainees will do a written project in which they focus their immediate ambitions - eg the kind of company they might like to run. Classwork is at their request. They decide what they want, and efforts are made to set up classes for them.

There is an opportunity to direct a full-scale production, usually one short play and they will also direct a public production (lunch-time) with third-year acting students. For this the directors are encouraged to do all their press and publicity work. The production will either be in the New Vic or in the Theatre Royal foyer. There is a budget of £120 for set and costumes and the production is later evaluated by staff.

One of the main strengths of the scheme is that it can capitalize on its direct links with a three-year acting course and a regional repertory theatre.

VII

c. Funding and Accreditation

A drama school may be a very suitable environment for training directors, but there is a tangle of funding problems that needs to be overcome before the system can work effectively. British students attend drama schools on discretionary grants, which create severe restrictions on the drama schools' selection of students. In fact, as the Drama Centre has found, directing students may fail to qualify for grants. With the size of the grant at the discretion of the applicant's local authority, some students will receive far less than others. Certain authorities give no discretionary grants at all to students accepted for drama schools. Then there are limitations on the number of grants given by an authority to each institution. The ILEA, for instance, has allowed London-based schools like RADA or Guildhall only one grant each. A further problem concerns students who have already graduated from a university. Because drama school courses are not recognized as being of postgraduate status (unlike some of the film and television school courses), those who have been through university are deemed to have used up their grant and must fund themselves if they want to pursue further study.

All these factors mean that, unless the drama school can offer a certain number of scholarships (as in the case of RADA), it will almost certainly be unable to take all the students it would wish to have. While it is well known that these problems are encountered by acting students, they affect would-be directing students even more severely, because they are more likely to have attended a university course first. Hence, the funding provisions need to be rethought so that this kind of training is not put at a disadvantage.

The situation will be further complicated by two other factors. Firstly, in London the abolition of ILEA will mean that each borough will be left to look after its own students, with the likelihood that discretionary grants will become even more scarce. Secondly, the proposed system of student loans will penalize directing students because the annual fees in drama schools are much higher than those in universities. (Compare a middle range school, the Guildhall School: £2,898 and £4,068 pa for foreign students, against a university postgraduate degree course, Leeds: £1,680 and £3,480 for foreign students.) At the same time the DES has stated that student grants will be frozen at present levels up till the introduction of the loan system in 1992. So the loans would probably be inadequate to cover the fees.

Any director training course in a drama school would need accreditation by the Conference of Drama Schools (CDS). Without this, students are unlikely to qualify for discretionary grants from local authorities. So as in the case of the Drama Centre and the Drama Studio, the course is limited to fee-paying students, who are not always the most talented.

The main obstacle here is that the CDS does not recognize one-year courses. Therefore, this ruling would need to be radically rethought by the CDS if drama schools are to play a serious part in director training.

d. How many Directors?

Both the Drama Studio and the Bristol Old Vic Theatre School have student directors taking part in classes alongside the acting students. The Drama Centre used a similar approach.

Two questions need to be considered here. Since a directing student would most probably not have passed the acting audition, is that director taking a place away from a more talented actor, or has the class been stretched? Also, is the rest of the class 'carrying' the director to any extent? This is relevant, because most drama schools reserve the right to throw out any student whose acting work does not progress satisfactorily.

For these reasons it seems that one or two directing students per class would be the maximum allowable. An alternative scheme is to take on more directors, say six or seven, and give them acting classes of their own. However, such segregation is not desirable as it goes against the very point of having actors and directors working alongside each other. With these numbers there would be enough for them to act in each other's productions. But this would create problems of space, a rare commodity in almost every drama school, with severely limited access to stage facilities.

e. To direct, or not to direct?

Any director training scheme in a drama school would encounter considerable opposition to the idea of trainee directors directing drama students. It would certainly not be advisable with first or second-year acting students, and while some directors we spoke to felt it might work with third-year students, the final-year productions of any drama school are so much a showcase for the actors that the choice tends to be limited to the most reliable directors.

3. Professional Courses and Schemes

a. British Theatre Association

The British Theatre Association (BTA) has been operating courses for directors for 40 years, though it remains heavily associated with amateur theatre. In recent years its activities have been hampered by cramped quarters and a lack of funds. At the time of writing the BTA faced the imminent probability of permanent closure.

Under the training programme organized by Victoria Thompson, it has catered for a variety of needs. These have varied from weekend courses on specific subjects (eg the voice, period movement, mime, obtaining sponsorship, children's theatre) to ten-day or two-week courses on periods of theatre (eg Shakespeare, contemporary theatre).

The main thrust of its director training programme had been a 13-week full-time course aimed at British amateur and professional directors, as well as foreign directors. The work has been mostly practical, giving experience of both acting and rehearsal problems. However, the wide age range (24 to 55), the diversity of backgrounds and abilities, and the fact that most students were working in English as a second language (only four British students out of 18), some with a very limited grasp of English, made it difficult to find a common language or way of working. Criticism by students themselves suggested that the course was trying to cover too much in too short a time, with the result that everything was superficial, fragmentary and unfocused. Also there was a feeling that the calibre of some of the teachers was not very high.

With the intention of overcoming these inadequacies, a one-year course was set up in the 1988-89 academic year. The first term was very similar to the 13-week course (with the same problems), the second term consisted of a placement in a London theatre or drama school to observe a production, while the third term was to be taken up with research work and rehearsal projects.

VII

123

In the event of the BTA closing its operation, it was intended that this one-year course would continue until the end of the academic year, though it seemed unlikely that there would any training beyond that. This is regrettable, because, although the standard of work may not have been the highest, the BTA did go some way towards counteracting any élitism which may exist in training whereby opportunities are open only to university students or those who had already proved their talent in the profession. Not only did it make director training accessible to all-comers, but it provided a valuable service to directors from Asian, African and South American cultures who might not normally have had access to training in Britain.

b. The Directors Guild

As so many directors have indicated, there is a great need for mid-career training, particularly cross-media training where, for example, directors with stage experience can get experience of television, or vice versa. The Directors Guild of Great Britain has approximately 900 working director members and it operates two schemes which are immensely popular and well received.

The first is the Observer Scheme which allows members to sit in on rehearsals for a particular production at their own expense. The initiative can come from either side: a director may contact the Guild inviting an observer, or a member may ask the Guild to try and set up an observing opportunity on a particular production. The Guild insists on CVs from members so that the host director can then make a final selection if several people apply for the one project. As well as plays both classical and contemporary, productions observed have included, films, television drama and opera. The period of observation has no limit; it can range from one day to several months. Although there is no formal monitoring of the scheme, reports from both sides have confirmed its success. In the Guild's view, the only shortcoming is that it is limited to directors who are themselves out of work and can afford to pay their own travel expenses and accommodation if necessary. Some kind of funding would allow at least expenses to be paid.

The second scheme is the Guild's Workshop Programme which usually provides opportunities for members to work on specialist areas with experts in the field. Subjects have included mime and physical theatre, puppet animation, performance art, working with actors, and television directing. There has also been a series of masterclass workshops conducted by directors such as Jonathan Miller, Michael Bogdanov, Gillian Lynne and Peter Brook.

The workshops are usually held at weekends lasting two or three days. They are held at the Actors Centre, London. Quite often those taking part will work as performers, but when actors are needed for directors to work with, professional actors from the Actors Centre have been invited to participate on a voluntary basis. The response from actors has usually been overwhelming.

The Guild would like to be able to organize longer workshops but feels that the cost would be prohibitive, considering that most directors have very low earnings. However, as it operates, the scheme appears to be a great success, providing one of the few opportunities where established directors, less-experienced directors and actors can all work together at a reasonably high level of professional skill.

c. The Centre for Performance Research, Cardiff

For over ten years the Cardiff Laboratory Theatre has earned a reputation for organizing some of the most stimulating international programmes of actor training in this country. That work is now continuing under the Centre for Performance Research and its director, Richard Gough, is seeking funding for a three-year modular programme of two-week workshops (about three modules a year) for directors. These would be conducted by directors of proven international status like Ariane Mnouchkine (France), Tadashi Suzuki (Japan), Peter Brook (France), Eugenio Barba (Denmark), Richard Schechner (USA), Jerzy Grotowski (Poland), Peter Stein (West Germany), Oleg Tabakov (USSR) and Richard Eyre (UK).

Each workshop would contract 12 professional actors for the two weeks. There would be places for eight experienced directors, and a further eight places for less-experienced directors who would have the status of assistants. Each participating director and assistant would work with a small group of actors to create a performance fragment or to realize a particular treatment. The teacher-director would work with each team, but a good part of each day would also be given over to group discussion, seminars, lectures and a form of masterclass.

A training programme on this imaginative level could have a very stimulating effect on the profession, benefiting actors as much as directors. And any form of training that will increase the international awareness of British directors is always to be welcomed. Furthermore, the Centre for Performance Research is one of the only organizations in this country with the contacts and the experience to set up such a programme.

VII

4. Bursaries and Attachment Schemes

Once a director has acquired the first level of training, a term of apprenticeship in a theatre (be it community theatre, TIE, regional rep or whatever) is widely seen as the best way into the profession. This often means a period of attachment as an assistant director. Even young directors with professional experience, or companies of their own, can still benefit from close contact with a senior director.

Of course the success of any attachment depends, first, on the calibre of the host director, second, on theatre's ability to give the trainee a worthwhile function, and third, on the trainee's capacity to make full use of the opportunity.

Since few theatres today can afford to pay an assistant director, the directors' bursaries and attachment schemes play a vital role in enabling this kind of training to continue. But there is a very serious gap here. Currently there are only 15 funded attachments in the whole of Great Britain:

BP Young Directors Festival	3
Regional Theatre Young Directors Scheme	4
Scottish Arts Council	4
Welsh Arts Council	2
Arts Council of Northern Ireland	2

The Arts Council of Great Britain currently offers no bursaries for trainee directors. It used to have four trainee bursaries each year and two or three associate bursaries. Under this scheme the applicant first had to get the sponsorship of the theatre company who then agreed to take responsibility for the training programme. Two references were also required. The training period was for one year, with a possible extension, and there was an expectation that the trainee would be given at least one major production to direct in the first year.

On a budget strained by the requirement to spread resources across the developing training needs of all art forms, the Arts Council Training Unit has been forced to cut out its Drama Trainee Director bursaries altogether. This it has done on the grounds that this area is at least partially provided for by other schemes, such as the RTYDS and BP Young Directors Festival (in which the Arts Council funds one bursary out of three).

A further reason given for the Arts Council change in priorities is that it perceives itself more and more as providing training opportunities in theatre for mid-career practitioners except where specific equal opportunities needs are being met. It has taken this position not only on grounds of the need to use reduced resources as wisely as possible, but because it perceives a positive need to support the career development of more established directors. At present, it is the only organization providing such support.

As a result the Arts Council's only director training scheme is for associate directors who want to prepare for their next move by becoming artistic directors. The focus of this bursary should therefore be as much on developing management skills and working in a large organization as on directing skills. It can be taken outside the theatre profession altogether, eg a local authority or in an institution abroad. This bursary is clearly most valuable, but has a very tight focus.

This does leave a serious gap in provision for new directors wishing to enter the profession. The Arts Council needs to consider carefully the long-term consequences of this, and to re-examine the whole question of training as a priority among its clients. For instance, it has been a policy that revenue-funded companies should spend a certain proportion of their budget on training, but so far this has never been properly monitored.

The Scottish Arts Council bursaries are for two trainees, who work as assistant directors in a theatre, and for two trainee associates who have more experience of directing professionally and can be expected to be given a freer hand when working with the host theatre.

a. BP Young Directors Festival

This scheme has been operating since 1987. It is funded by British Petroleum and administered by Battersea Arts Centre. The aim is to provide a showcase production with professional actors for each of the three winners who are then offered scholarships for attachments to selected theatres. It is limited to people aged 35 and under.

For the 1988 Festival there were 160 applicants (242 in 1987, 179 in 1989), shortlisted to about 50 on the basis of written submissions. This has tended to produce candidates of variable quality. As Ian Brown, one of the judges, wrote, "The problem in selecting from written text is that it is very difficult to know what written stimulus to give the potential candidate so that they will reveal the qualities of their mind, their sympathy and their understanding." It may also favour those who can express themselves vividly on paper.

The panel of judges (prominent members of the theatre profession) shortlists candidates. Over four days these directors are then assessed by the panel. Three directors each morning will rehearse a cast of student or young professional actors watched over by members of the panel who then interview them in the afternoon. Although this tends to reveal quite quickly the strengths and weaknesses of young directors, it is very easy for candidates to 'over direct' in order to impress the panel in a short time. There has been a tendency to butt in, or concentrate on irrelevant details that would normally be resolved towards the end of the rehearsal process.

After the selection weekend the three winners are each given the chance to rehearse a play of their choice for a two-week season at the Battersea Arts Centre before taking up their attachment.

VII

Ian Brown expressed reservations about the process adopted by the Young Directors Festival. He felt an assessment process that involved watching practical work and interviews was a perfectly sensible and useful technique, but it was not the ideal way, though that was very hard to define.

Although the Festival and its spirit are commendable, there are serious problems in the follow-up placements. It is left to the trainee to make contact with theatres and arrange the attachment. For those who are not prepared to leave London, this can pose problems. In fact, one of the participants in the 1988 Festival could not take up her follow-up attachment because she could not find a theatre that would take her. Also, the host theatre is expected to match the cost of the bursary, which means that it costs the theatre £3,000. There is no formal monitoring of trainees once they are on attachment. It was hoped that members of the panel would go and see trainees from time to time, but as the scheme could not pay travel expenses, and as members had heavy professional commitments of their own, there was little incentive to go.

b. Regional Theatre Young Directors Scheme

The Scheme is run by the Independent Television Fund on behalf of all the Independent Television companies. It is one of the most successful attachment schemes for directors - and the oldest - operating in this country. Since it began in 1960, over 130 trainees have passed through the Scheme. These include John Cox, Ken Loach, Adrian Noble, Barry Kyle, Bill Alexander, Michael Rudman, Giles Havergal, Pip Broughton, Trevor Nunn, Mike Ockrent, Debbie Shewell, Keith Hack, Dusty Hughes and Tim Albery, to name only a few.

There are three or four placements each year, open to directors between the ages of 20 and 26. The intention is that there should be continuous training for two years, the first year to be spent working in all departments of a theatre, both front-of-house and backstage. There may be the possibility of a production in the first year and, if the trainee is retained, a guarantee of at least two productions in the second year. Trainees are paid a fee equal to the Equity minimum for an assistant stage manager.

Much criticism has been levelled at the Scheme's age limit of 26 as this rules out more experienced theatre workers who may wish to change direction in their careers. At the same time it reinforces the 'bottleneck' pattern of early success referred to in Chapter III.

Serious problems were found in the Scheme's current selection process and the way that the successful candidates were matched up with theatres, which caused dissatisfaction on both sides. In 1988 the Scheme attracted 171 applicants (down from 230 the previous year). These were shortlisted to eight on the basis of a written submission giving personal details, practical experience and answers to questions designed to elicit their views on theatre practice. This shortlist comprised six men (including one Afro-Caribbean, one Asian) and two women. All were university-educated (two of them Oxbridge, three from drama departments). They were competing for four placements with theatres.

After the initial round of interviews, the selection panel and the artistic directors of the four receiving theatres (one artistic director was not present and was represented by the general manager) interviewed each candidate for 30 minutes. There followed a discussion between the panel and the artistic directors who then negotiated for their favoured candidates. Of the eight candidates, five were considered possible, with no support for the remaining three. Of the successful candidates, three were men (one Afro-Caribbean), one was a woman.

Hence the selection was based almost entirely on the way the candidates presented themselves, not on how they worked. No references were sought. The half-hour interviews seemed too brief to assess the candidates fully and the size of the interviewing panel (eight plus three observers) too large and intimidating. The absence of one artistic director, for whatever reason, was felt to be quite unacceptable. The composition of the selection panel itself seemed to have no clear logic in the range of expertise it represented.

Furthermore, there was no general agreement among artistic directors as to what degree of experience the trainee should receive during the two-year placement; for instance, whether they should be given a studio production in their first year or no production at all at any time. Also there is no formal means of monitoring progress and only incidental feedback at the end of two years.

It is felt that an overhaul of the Scheme is long overdue. There seems considerable disagreement over the kind of candidates for which it is designed, particularly over the question of experience. There seems little consistency in the kind of training offered. There are far too few places to meet the demand. The age limit of 26 unfairly excludes too many potential directors. The initial shortlisting process is hazardous. The composition of the selection panel needs reviewing.

However, it should be noted that the present administrator of the Scheme, Jack Andrews, took over only a year ago and already he is beginning to introduce a number of improvements. For instance, the monitoring of the scheme is much improved: Jack Andrews will visit trainees at their theatre whenever problems arise, and he also demands regular reports from both the trainee and the host theatre.

5. The National Companies

The Royal National Theatre was reviewing its director training policy at the time of our Enquiry. Richard Eyre: "The basis of taking on the education of directors is one more responsibility; of course the Royal National Theatre ought to have that responsibility. And we're trying to address ourselves to it, because we have the staff director system which is exemplary and essential because of understudies and because of looking after shows in repertoire. But it's absolutely incompatible with the training and encouragement of young directors. In the end aspiring directors aren't actually the best people to be staff directors; they need to be terribly patient and supportive and able to work with the understudies.

"We're stuck between that and occasionally having young directors working at the Studio. What I'd like to develop is some form of apprenticeship where every year we take on one or two directors and we take them through a year and we say that is part of the responsibility of being the Royal National Theatre."

Under the directorship of Peter Hall and later Trevor Nunn, the Royal Shakespeare Company had been successful in nurturing a new generation of directors through its assistant director schemes in the 1960s and 1970s. Some of those people are now running parts of the company. Whether the same provisions will exist for the next generation of RSC directors is hard to predict. There is evidence that fewer people of exceptional talent want to stay in positions of power with such a large company over a long term.

VII

Indeed, this is symptomatic of a wider problem: there is a dearth of suitably qualified people who want to be artistic directors. Understandably, many talented directors are unhappy with the burdens of the managerial role because it takes them away from the very thing they most enjoy doing, directing productions.

Trevor Nunn described what he had been trying to do. ''When I took over [the RSC in 1968] I was aware that there was a generation of associate directors all older than I was. Everything changed at the moment when we opened The Other Place. Then it became possible to institute a scheme of trawling for assistant directors, and we would interview up to 60 people, constantly insisting that we needed people of some experience and some achievement.

''We were not concerned with interviewing somebody who had never worked with professional actors. We were talking about the kind of attachment that would always include a production as well as being AD on a main-house production. Which would mean maintenance, understudy work, replacement work and so on. But not the system where there is just a house director who doesn't get directorial opportunities in other spaces. It was essential that these people did both. That was a conscious attempt to say here is somebody who is entirely unknown and, given the right amount of opportunitiy and nurturing and belief, and discussion, is going to deliver. And all of them did.''

As the national companies are theoretically the pinnacle, it could be argued that they should take on a more direct and thorough training role. But then the same case has been made - unsuccessfully - for them training actors. However, a stimulating programme of classes, workshops and projects has recently been taking place at the Royal National Theatre Studio under the direction of Peter Gill. Set up in 1984, the RNT Studio provides a place where new and experimental work of all kinds can be undertaken without the pressure of public performance. Apart from giving members of the RNT company opportunities to extend their skills through workshops and classes, it sets up extended projects involving a writer, a director and a group of professional actors, working either on a play, an idea or the adaptation of existing material. Although there is no pressure to show the work, the result is usually a workshop production, without costumes, scenery or lighting, to an invited audience. Some projects have subsequently been given full productions by the RNT or by other theatres.

Directors are also taken on attachment to the RNT Studio (usually for a period of three or four months) during which time they may have the chance to develop a project of their own choice, in addition to taking part in the classes and workshops. In the autumn of 1988 four young directors were attached to the Studio. Overall supervision is provided by Peter Gill and John Burgess.

Peter Gill emphasized the flexibility of the RNT Studio's approach. ''In five years we have undertaken to develop, not train, a number of directors. We've had Jenny Killick, Stephen Unwin, Nick Ward, Paul Miller, Jeremy Raison, Polly Teale, Tim Supple, Julia Bardsley and Decima Francis. We've done different things for different people. We've usually given them a project to do in a relaxed but professional atmosphere where they can call for help if they need it. But there is an expectation of certain standards.''

The value of the RNT Studio is that it offers not so much a training as a set of opportunities for directors to make a controlled leap from the haphazard conditions of alternative theatre to more professional practice. Some will find themselves casting for the first time, and this is one area where they are given close guidance. As Peter Gill said, ''To stop somebody casting the first person vaguely suitable for the part who doesn't frighten them is a real struggle for most young directors.''

6. Film and Television Courses

In contrast with director training for the theatre, the training in film and television seems to be reasonably well provided for. Indeed, the National Film and Television School (NFTS) operates a course comparable with any in the world. The main limitation appears to be the amount of attention courses give to working with actors and with writers.

The courses we visited were those at the London International Film School (LIFS), the London College of Printing (LCP), the National Film and Television School and the Royal College of Art (RCA). We also visited the course at the University of Bristol.

a. Student and Staff Profile

VII

Almost all the students in film and television schools are very clear about why they are there: they want to work in film and television. In most cases they will already have decided whether they want to be a director, an editor, a camera operator or whatever.

They are on the whole older than those who enrol in a drama department; usually in their mid-20s on entry, and highly motivated. Many of them will also have had professional experience of some kind, so they know the demands of the 'real world'. Their expectation will be of a vocational training that has close contact with the profession, and the course will endeavour to provide that at the highest level. (One exception is the London College of Printing which is technically a non-vocational course.) Indeed, we were impressed that several leading directors and producers regarded it as a vital part of their job to maintain contact with these training institutions. David Puttnam in particular has taken a very active role in training on several courses. To make a brief comparison with theatre, the senior directors of the national theatre companies did not appear to have close practical involvement with any drama school, or director training course. In fact they knew very little about them. This is another indication that the status of director training for the theatre is unacceptably low.

We also found that the film and television schools were more international in their outlook and had strong links with European film and film-makers, especially through the international film festivals in which students regularly take part. Staff were in touch with what was happening in Europe and the United States, and they would sometimes employ foreign directors according to availability. The feeling of a professional training was reinforced by the staff themselves. Almost all were working professionals, part-time or full-time.

Although the profession seems to discriminate heavily against women directors, there is evidence that most schools are trying to counteract this. LCP: 68% women, LIFS: 20% women, RCA: 30% women.

The London College of Printing consciously tries to encourage more women and has raised the proportion from 12% in 1984, to 68% in 1988. Its head of the Film and Television School, Haim Bresheeth, insists that this is not done out of positive discrimination. He still accepts the best people, but he has made an effort to let people know that there is interest. He found the average female applicant ''older, better qualified and more committed.''

Bresheeth was also aware that the College was getting very few black students. To counteract this he set up a one-year access course for the local community in Brixton. This has proved highly successful and he now finds that ''the people, black and white, from that access course are superior to the others.''

b. Selection

Students are usually chosen on the basis of submitted material (film, video or storyboard), written material and at a later stage, interview. As most of the courses run at a postgraduate level, applicants usually have a degree, though the schools do not insist on this if the talent justifies it.

One of the most thorough selection procedures is that of the London College of Printing. It was evolved by Haim Bresheeth from his research into film schools abroad. It is a three-year course without academic restrictions. To find 30 students, an initial selection is made from a reading of the 600 to 800 application forms. Of these, 300 are selected and sent a test pack in which they are asked to build a storyboard from 40 black and white images supplied. They also submit a short screenplay/treatment inspired by two of the images, and they write a critique of any film or television production they have seen. These returned submissions (about 80% of the total sent out) are screened by a panel composed of half staff and half students and about 100 applicants are selected for interview. References are also taken into account.

At the interview, conducted by two staff members and two students (second or third year), each applicant has 40 minutes; half of that time is for them to ask questions or show other work.

Since it was introduced, this system has produced a higher standard of student with virtually nil drop out rate during the course.

c. The Accent of the Training

Far from reproducing a broadly similar experience, there was a healthy variance of emphasis among the courses we visited. The London College of Printing, for instance, is concerned with producing independent film and television makers, with a particular interest in avant-garde and experimental work, rather than gearing students for mainstream BBC, ITV or commercial cinema.

The course at the Royal College of Art, on the other hand, places more emphasis on the commercial aspects of film-making. One of the first exercises students do is to make a promotional film or commercial. Significantly, many students on leaving go into the commercial sector, often making pop promos.

In the case of the Royal College, the pragmatic emphasis was partly in reaction to the type of work that was being produced before the present Head of the School, Dick Ross, took over in 1980: "There was every freaky movement in the place, with almost no-one wanting to make movies," he recalled. "With only one or two exceptions, the films that were made were just screaming polemic."

It was also partly due to pressure by the principal of the College, Jocelyn Stevens, who wanted to conform closely to the government's policy of encouraging a close relationship between industry and education. The achievement of Dick Ross has been to steer a successful middle way that enables students to develop their craft in a flexible environment, at the same time maintaining excellent relations with the film industry.

VII

What the courses tend to have in common is their emphasis on building a team in each intake, rather than taking a set of talented, but potentially incompatible individuals. This is seen as important as they will be expected to form production teams on each other's projects. Students tended to have a lot of unstructured time and seemed to work long hours. As one film student at the Royal College commented, "Most of us won't get out of here till 8 o'clock, and we work weekends as well. You work harder than on a structured course."

d. The National Film and Television School

The undisputed centre of excellence in film-training is the three-year course at the National Film and Television School, situated in the spacious film studios of Beaconsfield. Because of its national and international importance it deserves special attention.

Its principal is Colin Young and the philosophy of the School is to show that there are not so much rules as different ways of achieving results. The criterion for judging the work is not whether or not it is commercial, but whether the audience's attention will be held. The aim is therefore to reconcile flair and coherence.

First Year

The first two terms of the course are concerned with acting. All 30 of the students, whatever their specialization, take part in a series of practical exercises dealing with where you put the camera, how you use the actors and how you cast them. Pictorial exercises from the observed (working with a still camera, then a video camera in the local town) to the invented (working with actors) are used to lead students into fiction through the root of their observation of the world.

In the third term they are given a poem and asked to shoot an interpretation of it. At the end of this term they will also have experience of working on someone else's script. Most of the time students will be working on video, which is regarded as the initial training for cinema. Additionally, they will do varying multi-camera exercises.

Professional actors are brought in as required. There are also budgets for special tutors requested by the students. And there is money to book films for study, so that almost every day, a film is shown.

Second Year

The final two years are taken up with the students' own projects, not all of which go into production. The student director is encouraged to make at least two films in the second year, recruiting technicians from other courses. The student director is responsible for the budget and the productions are made without tutorial supervision of any kind, although the staff are involved in the post-production.

Third Year

The central project is a graduation film, again made in conjunction with technicians from other courses. Attempts are also made to get attachments for those who want them.

e. The Universities and the Profession

The Film and Television course at the University of Bristol is an excellent example of how contact between a university and the profession can be maintained. It runs under the directorship of John Adams.

In addition to television options at undergraduate level, Bristol runs a one-year intensive postgraduate course in Film and Television that aims to condense two years' work for those wishing to go into broadcasting or film. It also serves as a useful preliminary stage before going on to further training at a place like the National Film and Television School.

It can handle multi-camera video work through an exceptionally well-equipped studio, and single camera film or video work on location. A major aim of the course is to let students think conceptually about film and television in ways that would be impossible once they were in the profession.

Theory is taught only in so far as it leads into practice. The course takes 12 students (out of 400 applicants) and is one of the very few in the country to have ACTT recognition, which means that on graduating, the students automatically have ACTT union membership. Professional actors are sometimes used on projects (expenses paid) and there is a regular supply of established professionals for seminars and workshops.

As an adjunct, the Department runs a number of one-week courses each year for professionals, arranged with the Independent Television Association (in future to be known as the Independent Television Commission).

f. Working with Actors

"One of the things that gives away a novice director is that the performances are not believable." Colin Young

The short periods of engagement for which actors are usually required on a film or television project, and the enthusiasm of actors to gain experience of working in these media, means that the film and television schools have been able to find a neat solution to the problem of whom trainee directors work with.

In accordance with an Equity agreement, professional actors are engaged, with only their expenses paid - usually £20 per day. In the event of the film being subsequently sold, the actors are paid an appropriate fee. There appears to be no problem in finding actors; in fact the National Film and Television School has a long list of applicants to choose from. This solution usually works to the satisfaction of both sides, because among other things it allows actors the possibility of having an example of their work on video which they can show prospective employers.

VII

But inadequacies do occur in the amount of preparation that student directors receive. At the Royal College, for instance, student directors were thrown into their main project in which actors were involved before they had actually had any classes or workshops on how to work with actors. Although this was being rectified in the following academic year, it was a serious omission. As one directing student commented, ''The main problem is that the directors don't have respect for the actors. I've had one director who's been arrogant with every actor he's worked with.''

At one time, directing students from various schools did projects with acting students from drama schools. Although some of the film schools have expressed interest in continuing this relationship - Dick Ross in particular - the drama schools are not so keen. The head of one drama school said that the experience had not always used the students' time productively and projects were often set up in a disorganized way.

g. Who Writes the Film?

Approaches to directing fictional film are divided between the director as auteur and the director as interpreter of the writer. Each requires separate skills.

The London College of Printing concentrates on the auteur film-maker, students at the London International Film School are encouraged to script their own films. Students at the Royal College of Art all work as writers and tend to want to direct their own material, putting their 'my film' stamp on it.

The National School of Film and Television was in the process of developing its screenwriting course when we visited it, and staff were trying to steer directing students away from an exclusively director/writer approach. As Paul Dickson, Head of Direction, commented, ''We have discovered that if people would work on someone else's script, they would be better as directors than if they wrote themselves.''

Overall, directing students do not have enough work on text analysis and developing a script in conjunction with a writer. This is a particularly serious omission for those who will want to work in television where the director will be expected to work almost exclusively with a writer rather than work as auteur.

h. Entering the Profession

All the schools we visited recognized attachments with film or television productions companies as a highly desirable last stage to the training, and they made every effort to set these up. On the whole the profession is co-operative, and certain directors, like Richard Attenborough, make a point of regularly taking on a trainee.

The National Film and Television School does not seem to have much trouble finding placements for its students. The London College of Printing is only beginning to develop its placement programme. The London International Film School does not seem to have a strong programme of placements.

The Royal College of Art has been unsuccessful in placing students due to bad or non-existent relations with ACTT deriving from a long-standing disagreement. This also means that because ACTT does not recognize the course, no graduating student qualifies to join the union. However, students do not seem to have much difficulty entering the profession. In fact there is an 85% rate of employment when they leave.

Another important factor is that students from several of the colleges have had considerable success with their films at international film festivals. Within the profession festival prizes are highly regarded and they can provide an effective means of helping launch a young director's career.

136

i. Funding and Facilities

With the exception of the National Film and Television School, the courses we visited are operating in cramped and often compromising conditions. Studio space is limited and at the Royal College much of the equipment is outdated. Their work is almost totally on 16mm film since all video work has been in abeyance for three years because of the heavy cuts imposed on the course. Fortunately, Dick Ross has built up a strong rapport with the film and television industry who now subsidize the students to about 60%.

The London International Film School is the only privately-owned school. In the absence of any grant aid, it relies entirely on student fees. This means a high proportion of foreign students paying the higher rate. One or two British students have, however, managed to get local authority grants.

The National Film and Television School has, appropriately, excellent equipment and facilities that put it on quite a different level from anything else we have seen. It offers, in Colin Young's words, "the most costly training in Britain apart from pilots." Its overall budget for 1988-89 was £3.4 million. Similar costs per student are found in similar schools throughout Europe.

Enjoying complete autonomy from the DES, 51% of its budget comes directly from the Office of Arts and Libraries; 49% comes from the film and television industry. But this amount is now in jeopardy, pending the outcome of the government's White Paper on broadcasting. Many of the new Independent Television companies may have neither the funds nor the interest in putting large sums of money into training. This would leave the School with a huge funding problem; if it does not continue to be funded at this level, the course would have to close.

VII

7. Television Training

a. BBC Television Training

The BBC has given training a high priority since, in the early days, it was the only organization practising the art and craft of television. At that time training was an essential part of its self-perpetuation and propagation. That priority still survives today and, although in the long and recent past space and facilities were limited, the BBC's acquisition of Elstree Studios has allowed the development of a sophisticated training establishment.

The courses we are concerned with include one for production managers (equivalent to stage managers or first assistants in film) and this contains a strong directing element; a course for potential studio directors; and one for film directors, in a very general sense. The last course takes place six times annually, each of four weeks duration. They are essentially craft-based and embrace all aspects of television programming: drama, talking heads, documentary etc. One or two of the film courses each year are devoted specifically to documentary techniques. The students are all internal, nominated by various departments and finally selected by the TV Training staff. The exception is Light Entertainment which has a tradition of encouraging training and promotion from within the department.

The Drama Course is a fairly recent innovation and is designed specifically to train potential drama directors to work in film and video, in the studio and on location. Again, there is a strong craft element since some of the students will be external with no direct experience of the workings of film and TV.

Selection for this course is quite different. Each BBC drama controller around the country can submit names - internal and external. The latter occurs if, say, a theatre director working in Scotland applies to Bill Bryden (Controller of Drama, Scotland) who might put him/her forward ahead of his own staff application - subject to talent and potential. The final numbers are eight per course, two courses per year. On the last two courses, six were external students, mostly from the theatre, and one writer. This final number has to be negotiated and agreed by the drama heads, then TV Training is presented with the final eight.

The course lasts ten weeks and is very practical, with several exercises on multi-camera video and film. Highly-esteemed actors are used throughout. Six weeks are devoted to video, four to film. External students come onto the courses two weeks earlier for a period of familiarization.

The school insists that the training is for the profession and not for the BBC's exclusive use. In drama the 'after-care' consists of no more than the postgraduate student attempting to persuade a producer that he/she is ready and able. Series and Serials offer each student six episodes of *East Enders* as a first bite at the real cherry.

There are four staff tutors, together with a large number of outside professionals for tutorials, workshops, critiques etc. There is no policy of positive discrimination, merit and potential being the only criteria. However, recent courses included one black and several women students.

There is no specific part of the course devoted to working with actors - although theatre directors will have had that experience and most internal students will have been witness to the process through their previous positions. A suggestion that an actor used as a teacher, to discuss the actors' problems rather than just attend as camera-fodder, was noted with interest.

Working with writers will be introduced via the appointment of a script editor to the tutorial staff in a consultancy capacity.

Clearly the BBC provides an important benchmark since it does have enormous experience in the art and craft of television and consequently in its training requirements.

b. Independent Television Companies

The short courses at the University of Bristol have been referred to. Throughout the independent sector, director training is limited and usually geared to fill vacancies as they arise. The director training at Scottish Television is a good example. Each of the directors will be given a training period of about six months. They are allocated to different departments in turn and during that time their particular strengths are assessed. Though they would not be immediately assigned to departments, of last year's two trainees, one director was taken on to work exclusively in drama and the other went into current affairs. Increasingly, however, Independent Television companies are relying on using freelance directors who have had their training and initial experience elsewhere.

Summary

Theatre

On the courses and schemes we visited we saw various components of training, but no one institution has attempted a complete training for directors.

The drama departments of universities and polytechnics play an indispensable role in the training of theatre directors in that they are supremely equipped to provide the theoretical and cultural background, along with a certain amount of practical work. But because of the academic emphasis, the practical aspects are skimmed over and students end up with a shallow grasp of acting and directorial skills, and very few opportunities to direct a full production.

VII

Overall contact with the profession is extremely poor, though it must be said that professional theatres have shown little interest in forging links with universities. This should be corrected. At the same time, many students we spoke with showed a noticeable lack of drive and enthusiasm. One reason given was a feeling of pessimism about the state of the arts in general. The proposed loans system is likely to have an adverse effect on the intake of students because of the uncertain employment prospects in the theatre.

A director training course located in a drama school can provide a higher standard of actor training and the chance to work alongside actors. But there will not necessarily be a chance to direct the acting students.

A solution tried by the Old Vic Theatre School was to run parallel courses in which directors occasionally merged with the actors. But most drama schools today are severely hampered by space problems. However, the Drama Studio in Ealing seems to operate a commendable course at postgraduate, post-experience level, though it would be even better if it were properly funded.

The haphazard system of grants for drama students, and the non-accreditation of directing courses by the CDS, is unsatisfactory and needs radical revision if drama schools are to play a significant part in director training.

Training opportunities at professional level are scarce and need to be opened up. The BTA courses have serious limitations, and we understand they are closing due to lack of funds. The Directors Guild Observer Scheme seems an excellent way to facilitate access to the profession and there is also a great need for the kind of opportunities provided by its Workshop Programme. Both schemes could be usefully expanded and they deserve adequate funding. Alternatively, they could be taken over by an independent co-ordinating body of the kind described in Chapter IX. The opportunities for contact with leading foreign directors are almost non-existent, which is why a scheme like that of the Centre for Performance Research, Cardiff deserves support.

The number of bursaries and attachment schemes for trainee directors is far too low for the demand. These offer an essential training experience that needs to be made more widely available. Training priorities within the Arts Council and other funding bodies need to be carefully re-examined. The BP Young Directors Festival and the RTYDS are excellent in their intentions and provide invaluable training opportunities. The Young Directors Festival however is not funded to monitor the placements which follow from it and the selection procedure used by the RTYDS rules out older applicants. The placements following the Young Directors Festival are insufficiently funded so that theatres have to pay half the costs, which in turn narrows the choice of willing theatres.

Both the Royal Shakespeare Company and the Royal National Theatre should increase their commitment to director training as this influences their supply of new directors. The RSC relies solely on its assistant director system, though the National has developed a more flexible and less pressured way of nurturing directors through its Studio.

Film and Television

The film and televison schools are able to operate on a more professional level of training with more mature students who are clearer about their vocational goals. The best of these courses are very well thought out and they provide a thorough foundation. There is also close contact with the profession and an admirable commitment to training on the part of the film and television industry. Most of the schools have strong links with European film-makers and some of them maintain a high profile abroad through their successful participation in international film festivals.

The schools show a healthy diversity of approaches, from highly experimental to more commercially-orientated film-making. When needed, they are able to employ professional actors, though the areas of neglect tend to be inadequate preparation for working with actors or understanding the acting process, and insufficient attention paid to the process of developing a script in collaboration with a writer. This is partly because the slant of most courses is towards the writer/director.

Several of the schools arrange attachments for their students whereby they can join a professional film production. Some of them have ACTT recognition which facilitates entry into the profession.

The National Film and Television School course is highly respected within the international film industry and is well-funded. However its future may be uncertain if the new Independent Televison companies decline to support it.

The other schools are often hampered by limited funds, which revealed inadequate working conditions and which affects their production output. It should also be noted that there are hardly any high-standard film courses operating outside London.

Television

The training of television directors within the profession relies heavily on the BBC's courses. Although its ten-week drama course is of a high standard, the approach to working with actors is once again skimmed over. More time and attention should be given to this.

The recently published White Paper on Broadcasting is conspicuous for many things, not least for its total failure to mention any form of training needs or responsibilities for the future. Given the market-led philosophy of the proposals, it is not surprising that training has no priority, however short-sighted and finally self-defeating that omission might prove.

VII

Director training amongst the Independent Television companies is sporadic and in jeopardy because of the increasing use of freelance directors and uncertainties over the funding of individual companies. There is a heavy reliance on the short professional courses run for the ITC at the University of Bristol.

Overall, the training for film and television is relatively well-provided for and there exists a healthy state of contact between training institutions and the profession. But the training in theatre is unsatisfactory on many levels: it lacks depth or thoroughness, it lacks the respect and support of the theatre profession, and it lacks an overview whereby the standard of work can be assessed. Universities, polytechnics and drama schools have an important role to play in training directors, but at present their potential is far from fulfilled.

Significantly, when we asked those directors who were trained how they rated their training, film and television directors gave a much more positive response than theatre directors.

TABLE 12 - QUALITY OF TRAINING

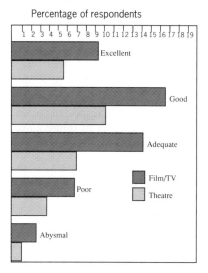

Percentage of respondents

Chapter VIII

TRAINING SOLUTIONS ABROAD

VIII

In order to make comparisons with director training courses abroad we were reliant principally on written evidence from the institutions themselves and on comments from people who had either studied, directed or taught abroad.

1. Theatre

There are many examples, both on the Continent and in the United States, where the training of directors is highly developed. In almost all cases the training is conducted through drama schools or universities.

In Germany, Czechoslovakia, Rumania, Poland and the Soviet Union, director training is rigorous and very closely linked to the profession. The training is also geared to the different role that the director fulfills, which is not necessarily compatible with practices in Britain. In West Germany, for example, as Peter Hall found, it is not acceptable for a director to say "I don't know." There is an expectation that the director will invariably have all the answers and that the actors must do as they are told.

Terry Hands was once asked why he would never invite someone like the Italian director, Giorgio Strehler to do a production for the RSC. "Giorgio is a friend but I wouldn't bring him within ten miles of the RSC," said Hands. "He does every gesture. It's drill, morning, noon and night. My people would just get nervous breakdowns, or kill him." Playwrights have also found it difficult to accept the way Continental directors work. Arnold Wesker suggested that because the director is supreme on the Continent, "writers have been frightened from the scene knowing their plays will never be realized as they conceived them.

"A madness is sweeping through European theatre," he continued. "It is a madness which has elevated the role of the director above the role of writer. The stage has become shrill with the sounds of the director's vanity; it has become cluttered with his tricks and his visual effects. The productions we are seeing claim attention to himself rather than attention to the play. The playwright's vision of the human condition has become secondary to the director's bombastic striving for personal impact; his text is cut, re-arranged, distorted, or ignored by the director and sometimes by the actors.

"We are no longer invited to see Shakespeare's *King Lear*; we are invited to see, perhaps Strehler's *King Lear*. It is not Eugene O'Neill's *Hairy Ape* that was recently produced in Germany, it is Peter Stein's *The Hairy Ape*."

In the Soviet Union, Brian Cox observed that there were often two directors on a production, just as Stanislavsky and Nemirovich Danchenko had often worked together. One would be responsible for the mise-en-scène, the other would rehearse the actors. Jean Benedetti was impressed by the new diversity of work in the Soviet Union; pre-perestroika, both the training and the work had been extremely rigid. He also noted the rapport directors had with actors. "If you walk into a Russian rehearsal, they're not having any trouble communicating because they're all using the same language."

Initial training on the Continent is sometimes followed by a long apprenticeship. As Tim Albery noted while directing opera in West Germany, a trainee director might assist one particular director for four or five years before being given a production to direct. This means that there are almost no young directors working in the profession.

a. Poland

Poland has two state drama schools which run directing courses, in Warsaw and Cracow. Both are financed by the state. A description of the director training course at the Higher Theatre School of Warsaw will give an idea of how training is structured in Eastern Europe.

There are 37 teachers on the staff, several of whom work exclusively in the Directing Department, but most of whom teach in the rest of the school or work in the profession. The intake is between 4 and 6. So over the 4 years of the course there is a total of 16 to 24 students in the faculty. Admission is on merit ad is not influenced by gender, social position, race or nationality. The age limit on entry is 32.

Student directors study for three years at the school, then spend their third year on attachment to a professional state theatre in which they will have the chance to direct. The degree of control in the profession is high: the only way to get a directing licence in Poland is to be accepted by the Academic Commission.

For the first two years at the school students will direct acting students from the drama department. But during their third year they will direct productions with professional actors. Also, during their second and third years they spend a certain period of time on attachment to theatres as assistant directors. In the course of their training they will have at least 12 seminars with top Polish directors.

The elements that are taught include technical problems of staging, scenography and theatre architecture, history of stage design, text analysis, theatre of Shakespeare and Molière, sociological and psychological analysis of text, the history of dance and the study of manners and customs, the problems of stylized or non-conventional acting (finding a reality in that), the history and theory of music, and use of music in performance, seminars on the literature of different periods (Polish romanticism, the Biblical tradition, *The Odyssey* and *The Illiad*) the history of drama, philosophical studies and the anthropology of theatre.

VIII

While this training is clearly very thorough and systematized, its disadvantage is that it could produce directors who think along the same lines instead of developing their own.

b. Soviet Union

Edward Braun visited Moscow in April, 1989 and made the following observations:

In the Soviet Union the training of directors is shared amongst six theatre schools, three of them in Moscow and one each in Leningrad, Kiev and Minsk.

Foremost amongst them is the State Institute of Theatre Arts (GITIS) in Moscow. The course at GITIS lasts five years, with 20-25 students graduating each year. Of these an average of five will have trained as directors. There are 15 full-time staff, plus part-time assistants including prominent working directors. Acting and directing students, in a ratio of about 4:1, work together throughout the course, and for the past two years there has also been a small number of students engaged purely in theory and criticism.

The age at entry varies between 18 and 30, with considerable importance attached to previous 'life experience' rather than formal qualifications. The selection process extends over a full year, with GITIS staff travelling throughout the country, interviewing candidates and viewing their work. Aspirant directors are expected to show some acting potential, though not necessarily proven acting ability. A few students are recruited from abroad, and need not necessarily speak Russian when they first enrol. Arrangements exist for the affiliation of extra-mural students, working elsewhere in the Soviet Union and visiting GITIS periodically to present work in progress.

At GITIS there has been no formal curriculum since 1981, and a range of skills, both technical and personal is developed through project work. The main emphasis is on work with the actor. There is considerable freedom in the choice of dramatic texts for exercises, though students are expected to work 'in accordance with the author's intentions.' Devised work and improvisation are also regular features. The average week includes 30 hours of course work, breaking down into three seven-hour days plus movement and dance sessions. Each session lasts two hours. The precise composition of the programme will vary according to the staff in charge of a particular year.

Little emphasis seems to be placed on the theoretical writings of Stanislavsky, Meyerhold or Vakhtangov on the directing courses at GITIS, even less on Socialist Realism (described as a 'false programme'). The theoretical/historical side of theatre is acknowledged as a relative weakness of the course. The main emphasis is placed on the development of individual creativity. One of the senior staff commented, ''I don't believe in conformity; even in the Party there's no conformity. Consensus is another matter - the acknowledgement of mutual dependence.''

Final-year directing students present a diploma production with professional actors in a Moscow theatre. Very few fail to graduate and there is little difficulty in securing regular work in one of the numerous theatres throughout the USSR.

c. United States of America

In the United States director training takes place through the universities. There are no drama schools that train directors. Almost every young director therefore has a Bachelor of Fine Arts (BFA) or a Master of Fine Arts (MFA). There is not a strong contact with the profession, with few provisions for attachment to theatres. Directing students direct each other as part of their training, not professional actors.

With a very large number of universities throughout the United States offering courses in directing, the standard appears to be extremely uneven. Some graduates said they had learnt little of practical help. At the same time, a few courses have international reputations.

Yale University's four-year course is currently regarded as one of the best. In a drama department of 200 students, there is an annual intake of four directing students (thus 12 over the four years: five men and seven women). Of the 84 applicants for the directing course in 1988-89, 56 were men and 28 were women. With the exception of one Canadian, all of those accepted were Americans. The average age was 28.

One of the most respected courses is that at Carnegie-Mellon University in Pittsburg. Mike Alfreds studied there and found it "excellent, intensive and organized most efficiently." Since no comparable model exists in Britain, his description of the course is worth printing verbatim:

* The department provided courses for all theatre practitioners: actors, designers, playwrights, stage managers, technicians and directors.

* Directing students were required to take all the courses available in acting (the first two years), design, technical work, (the first year), playwrighting and theatre management (the second and/or third year).

* All directors - all students, in fact - had to participate on set and costume construction, to be part of sound, lighting and stage crews. Directors had also to stage manage and assistant direct. All this was in connection with Main House productions directed by faculty members. Those shows were quite elaborate. Directors also had to act in them.

VIII

* Directing classes only started in the second year; in the third year, directing students directed one one-act play each semester; in the fourth year, they directed a full-length production.

* There were six Main House productions a year, as I mentioned above, directed by faculty members or guests; approximately four graduate productions (full); and almost every fortnight a triple bill of one-acts throughout the year, done with a minimum of production means.

* All students had to attend all these productions which formed the basis for very strenuous sessions of analysis and criticism in most classes (acting, directing etc).

* In addition, there was an endless stream of scenes prepared for class work.

* Acting was taught in three parallel strands by teachers whose philosophies and approaches were very different; often apparently in direct conflict with each other. There were voice and movement classes.

* In design class, directors learned to make ground plans, perspective drawings, colour wheels, models, etc.

* In the playwrighting class everyone had to write at least one play.

* In text analysis class we had for two years to read one play a week and write a critique and synopsis.

* The average day went from 8.30 am to 11 pm. Mornings were devoted mainly to academic classes (history of theatre, text analysis etc) and theoretical studies; afternoons to acting classes, rehearsals, scene work etc; evenings to crew work, rehearsals and performance.

* In directing classes the first year was devoted mainly to understanding the mechanics of staging: why and how you designed a ground plan in a certain way, the creating of focus, balance, picturization, contrast; the aesthetics of mass, line, colour etc; how to move groups of people on stage etc. The remaining years concentrated on the practical carrying out of interpretation, the understanding of conventions (style) and genres (comedy, farce etc) - ie we had to be able to justify our choices.

* During the last two years directing students were required to write papers on tragedy, melodrama, farce, comedy; to write reviews of plays, of operas, of other musical events, of novels, of art exhibitions, to research and give an illustrated lecture on one historic period of theatre (eg Jacobean) and one artistic movement in theatre (eg naturalism). As our 'thesis' - in addition to our actual physical production - we had to prepare a 'complete' performance of another play on paper, with designs, a prompt book with staging, essays on the cultural background of the author, on interpreting the play itself, on character analysis.

* From the acting classes we learned about different approaches to acting (Stanislavsky, Brecht etc), about rehearsal processes and we also were taught a lot about improvisation.

''I have gone into a lot of detail because I wanted to convey the comprehensive and intensive as well as intense, nature of the training. The amazing thing, looking back and comparing the attitude of actors and drama students training in the UK, was that we were able to cope with this huge work load. No-one complained of being tired or wanting 'time off'. In fact many students managed to create additional projects on their own outside the framework of the official course. The emphasis was constantly on learning crafts and becoming skilful at your job. Art was offered as something to aspire to through the attainment of craft.

"It's pretty self-evident that this sort of training requires a facility which can provide space, time and of course, money. It also requires a highly organized group of instructors to inter-relate in the smooth running of a complex schedule. I might point out that then the department had only two performance spaces; one, the main stage for faculty and graduate student productions and the studio. Stages were extremely well-equipped.

"Of course, this programme was designed before the concepts of TIE, community theatre, group-created pieces, performance arts, etc were prevalent or fashionable. But it seems to me that its structure was open to absorb new ideas about theatre as they appeared. (I write of it in the past tense as I have no idea what the programme contains now.) I know that I came out of this training with a huge amount of knowledge, both theoretical and practical. I felt very confident to pursue a career."

At a professional level the American Directors Institute (ADI) runs an active programme of workshops including its annual American Directors Conference at the Eugene O'Neill Theatre Centre. Ten professional directors are selected by a panel from the ADI's Directors Advisory Council, and these people will rehearse a production with professional actors, designers and technicians over the three weeks of the conference. Each piece has the equivalent of six days rehearsal and it gets two staged readings before an audience. There are discussions and critiques after each of the showings. The rehearsal process is also augmented by seminars, at least twice a week, led by invited master directors.

The ADI has also helped spread information on training through the publication of its *American Directors Sourcebook* which includes the data of a survey on directors, career information, contacts and training opportunities. Apart from the present report no such information on director training exists in Britain.

A particularly valuable training opportunity was provided by the British American Arts Association in 1987 when it offered scholarships to three established British theatre directors to carry out research or study in the United States. There was a reciprocal arrangement for Americans to visit Britain. For the three British directors, David Gothard, Philip Headley and Joan Knight, it marked an important point in their artistic development. More high-level scholarships of this kind would be a very effective means of providing stimulus for senior directors.

2. Film and Television

a. EEC Countries

National film and television schools in the EEC are lavishly funded on a scale that, in Britain, is matched only by the National Film and Television School at Beaconsfield. In 1987 Haim Bresheeth visited schools in

Copenhagen, Berlin, Munich, Brussels and Paris. Our comparison of these courses is based on his report.

The schools were: Den Danske Filmskole, Copenhagen (DDF), Deutsche Film und Fernsehnakademie Berlin (DFFB), Hochschule fuer Fernsehn und Film Munchen (HFFM), Institut National Superieur des Arts du Spectacle et Techniques de Diffusion, Brussels (INSAS) and Fondation Européenne des Metiers de L'Image et Son, Paris (FEMIS). FEMIS is the most recent school; it was set up in 1986.

The length of the courses varies from up to five years (at HFFM) to one and a half years (FEMIS). Students are usually around 25 on entry and the proportion of women directors in the intake varies from a quarter (HFFM) to a half (DFFB). A certain number of places are usually open to foreign students: at the HFFM, a quarter of the intake is foreign.

The schools operate a range of departments. For example at the DDF there are five areas of specialization: direction, camerawork, editing, sound and production. On average, each school will take between 10 and 15 directing students and there are ample opportunities for production work using excellent and up-to-date facilities. FEMIS differs from the others in that it sees itself not as a film and television training establishment but as an 'image and sound' teaching institution. The division between film and video is therefore less pronounced.

Although all the schools have state funding, several of them have faced financial cuts in recent years and have been increasingly engaged in tough negotiations to preserve their annual budgets. The funding of FEMIS deserves special mention as it operates on a system broadly similar to that of the National Film and Television School in Beaconsfield. 20% of its budget comes directly from the film and television industry, 40% comes from the Ministry of Culture and Communication and 40% is from a levy on the exhibition of films (similar to the now-defunct Eady levy in Britain). By 1995, it is planned to finance 30% of the annual operating costs from income that will be earned by the School through the sale of completed films and video productions and through special commissions. The modernization of film and video training in France, under the last government, has led to the planning of a whole system of regional training centres, with the heart of the system in Paris, as FEMIS.

b. Poland

The Higher State Film School in Lodz produces about 80% of Poland's film directors as well as many of its television directors. Since it was founded in 1948 it has turned out over 250 directors including Andrzej Wajda and Roman Polanski. Its curriculum was initially based on Soviet and French models, but was later adapted to suit the needs of Polish culture, and it eventually developed a teaching style of its own. The School is funded by the State and has good support from the film and television industry. The teaching staff comprise top professionals. Actors, cameramen and producers are also taught at the School.

In addition to the four-year course for directors, the School also runs short refresher courses for professional film and television directors.

c. United States of America

Almost 700 American institutions offer programmes in film, televison and radio. The courses are offered as part of a degree in Communications. Often, because of the university context, there will be close contact with the training of actors. It is interesting to note the emphasis placed on acting in these courses. The Californian Institute of the Arts had this to say about its directing students: ''Acting Studio experience is considered essential - not because we expect students to develop the full range of performing skills, but because as a director it is important to have a first-hand experience of the actors' problems. Some experience in acting is also, we believe, an invaluable background for dramatic writing.''

One of the problems of film training in the United States is that it is easily dominated by the commercial values of the huge Hollywood industry. A viable alternative has been developed by the Sundance Institute under Robert Redford. Operating in a similar fashion to the American Directors Institute workshop at the O'Neill Centre, it takes on 14 directors and helps them develop film projects during three weeks of workshops under the guidance of master directors and scriptwriters. Some of these directors will be working solely on their scripts, others will concentrate on the pre-production work, with opportunities to shoot scenes. Several projects worked on at the Institute have subsequently gone into full production.

VIII

PART THREE

THE WAY FORWARD

Chapter IX

TOWARDS A BETTER TRAINING IN BRITAIN

IX

The solutions put forward in this chapter emphasize theatre because that is where the training for directors is seriously inadequate. However, insofar as the experience of directing plays on stage is often a first step towards directing in opera, film, television or radio, most of our comments will also be relevant to those media.

In this chapter we will consider two broad options which are not alternative but should co-exist: basic training and post-experience training.

1. Basic Training

Many people will be starting out with no training whatsoever and therefore will be looking for a more practical alternative than a degree in drama.

As far as theatre training for directors is concerned, there appears to be no one institution that offers a complete vocational training. All that exists at the moment is bits and pieces of training that cannot pretend to go into any serious depth. Some institutions are at present doing the right things, but not doing them well. Some should not be attempting what they are doing because they are not equipped for it, through a lack of facilities, staffing or funding.

The National School of Film and Television could be cited as an example that does work. But its costs are huge and its students have usually done their initial training in a university, so they are older (average age on entry is 26) and will have taken altogether six years of study. Furthermore, while film training can be contained in one location, such as the studio complex at Beaconsfield, theatre training, at present, needs to draw on different institutions: drama departments, drama schools and theatres.

Ideally, what is needed is at least one consistently conceived, thorough training course that will address itself to the full range of skills a theatre director requires at a level equal to the best training abroad. This can only happen in a school that offers training in all the departments of theatre because a director cannot train properly without access to actors, designers, stage managers and so on. Until such a course is set up the problems of director training in Britain will never fully be solved.

However, under the present cultural climate it is unrealistic to expect this to happen in the near future. For one thing, no existing institution could house such a course. Also, it would require vast funding, even to cater for a very limited number of student directors. That is why the modular option for post-experience training is put forward as an interim solution.

a. The Three Year Professional Course

If a three-year course at postgraduate level were set up - a theatre-equivalent of the Beaconsfield model - what could be realistically achieved? In the absence of a complete theatre school, this could be split into three locations within a particular city; these would be a drama school, a university, polytechnic or college and a theatre. The course would need to be flexible enough to allow for someone who was experienced in one area of the training to by-pass that and concentrate on the other areas.

First Year

This would offer three optional areas of work. Students would choose one of these depending on their previous experience:

i) The Academic Background

This would be organized by the drama department of a university, polytechnic or college.

ii) The Acting Process

This would take place in a drama school. The directing students would go through the process that the First Year actors go through, with no more than one director in each class. There would also be the opportunity for a certain amount of instruction in the technical background, provided by the school's stage management department.

iii) The Technical and Managerial Background

The technical aspects of this option would be provided by the stage management department of a drama school, or alternatively, by a school of theatre design. The managerial side could be provided by a university or other suitable institution.

Second Year

In the second year the course would be attached either to a drama department or to a drama school, though it would run autonomously. Having completed their options, all the students would come together for the first time to study the rehearsal process and the elements of stage craft. As this would be essentially practical, there would be ample opportunity to direct scenes and plays. At first the students might direct each other, but this is not an ideal solution and at some point there should be the involvement of professional actors and the chance to do a full-scale production with them.

Third Year

Each student would be attached to a theatre. During this period, the apprentice director would have experience of all the departments involved in running a theatre, and would spend a considerable period of time assisting the director in rehearsals. Towards the end of the attachment the apprentice would be guaranteed at least one production in the theatre.

b. Making it Happen

With a certain amount of restructuring of provisions, this system could be set up regionally to cater for, say, two directors in each region. However, in the second year, when students would work together, the various regional courses might have to be combined to provide a sufficiently large group, say eight people. The following examples show how the regional networks might be set up:

Bristol:	Bristol Old Vic Drama School
	University of Bristol Drama Department
	Bristol Old Vic Theatre
Manchester:	Manchester Polytechnic (drama school)
	University of Manchester Drama Department
	Manchester Royal Exchange Theatre
London:	Guildhall School of Music and Drama
	Goldsmiths' College
	Young Vic Theatre
Glasgow:	Royal Scottish Academy of Music and Drama
	University of Glasgow
	Citizens Theatre
Cardiff:	Welsh College of Music and Drama
	University College of Wales at Aberystwyth
	Theatr Clwyd

Any such course should not be biased in favour of school-leavers, but should be appropriate for mature students and people who have worked in the profession. Non-standard entry is fundamental to this approach. Under the present funding structures radical changes will have to take place before such a system can operate.

2. Post-Experience Training

Most directors have agreed that it is possible to make an initial splash at the age of 20, but good direction needs life experience which can only come with the years. So we must evaluate life experience alongside technical training. At the same time it should be recognized that there are still things to learn at 45. Training must be seen as a continuing element in a professional life, not as something that is done in one bite at the outset: one advantage is that directors will be better able to respond to the changing conditions of theatre throughout their long careers. For example, theatre management skills were not a particularly demanding aspect of an artistic director's job 20 years ago: they are today. Mime and physical theatre were not as widely utilized in the theatre 10 or 15 years ago: they are today and many directors would benefit from knowing about them.

What directors must do is to be aware of the gaps in their own training. Funding bodies and the education sector must also acknowledge this and help bring about the circumstances whereby the gaps can be filled and the training completed.

a. The Modular Solution

A modular system of training, whereby people can fill the gaps and undertake further training as they perceive the need, offers a realistic short-term solution. The nature of the modular approach is that elements of training (modules) can occur at any point in a professional life.

What is needed now is for directors to look at their own experience and identify where the gaps are. For example, someone who has done a single Honours Drama degree, and has done production work, may need an attachment. Someone who has trained as an actor may need to study the theoretical background. If this concept is accepted, then clearly the way ahead is through:

i) a co-operative sharing of resources between drama departments, drama schools and theatres, and

ii) a network of flexible training opportunities at professional level. To test how this might work let us take a few hypothetical case histories.

b. Case Histories

i) The experienced actor

Jill is a successful actor in her 40s who wants to change course and concentrate on directing. She has worked with a variety of directors in classical and modern theatre, as well as having experience of film and television.

She has the acting background and a sound working knowledge of stage-craft. The main gaps in her training are the theoretical background and the experience of directing actors.

She takes an attachment to a theatre for one year where she concentrates on the technical background and informally studies the theoretical background while working as assistant director on a number of productions. During this time she is given a studio production of her own.

ii) The freelance director

George is a freelance director in his late 30s who wants to make the transition to opera. He has a thorough experience of directing plays of all kinds and some theoretical knowledge.

The gap in his training is a working knowledge of opera production and the cultural background to opera.

IX

He spends a year on attachment to an opera company, informally studying the cultural background while assisting directors on various productions and being present at all stages of the work, from initial discussions with the conductor through to the orchestral dress rehearsals. During the year he is given a revival to direct in collaboration with the resident staff director.

iii) The teacher

Cathy is a university lecturer in her 30s who wants to become a professional director. She has a sound knowledge of the theoretical background, but little practical experience of directing.

The gaps in her training are a practical knowledge of working with actors, a working knowledge of the technical aspects of theatre production, and the experience of directing.

She takes a special one-year course attached to a drama school with a first year acting class, as well as attending classes in stage management.

Following that she is given a one-year attachment to a theatre. She assists on productions and pays particular attention to all the aspects of running a theatre, backstage and front-of-house. During the year she is given a production of her own.

After a few years of successful freelance work she wants to apply for the artistic directorship of a regional repertory theatre. The gaps in her training are the management and administrative skills.

She takes a three-month course on management skills and spends a further month with a regional arts association gaining a thorough knowledge of arts funding. She then spends two months with a regional repertory theatre directing a production for part of the time, but also working closely with its artistic director. She sits in on board meetings, and meetings with funding bodies.

iv) The novice

Michael is 18 and has just left school with three A levels. He wants to work in the theatre and thinks he would like to direct. He is starting from scratch.

He enrols in the drama department of a university or polytechnic where he spends three years learning the cultural and theoretical background, and also gaining a certain amount of experience being directed by and directing his fellow students.

On graduating he takes a one-year course in a drama school where he gains a more thorough experience of the acting process.

After leaving the drama school, he forms a small company of his own, doing mainly small-cast plays in pub theatres. Two years later, he does a one-year attachment in a theatre, working as assistant director and paying particular attention to the backstage and other technical aspects of mounting a production. During this year he is given a studio production to direct.

Alternatively, on the completion of his drama degree, he does two years in a professional directing course (basic training) - if it existed.

v) The established director

John, in his 40s, is a respected associate director of a regional repertory theatre. He wants to learn more about lighting and he also wants fresh stimulus in approaches to directing.

He leaves the theatre for four months and spends a month observing and working with a leading lighting designer. He spends a further two months attached to an experimental theatre company and watches them develop a devised production. During his time with the company he gives one or two workshops, passing on his own skills. He then spends a further month taking part in a master class workshop conducted by a visiting international director.

c. The Requirements

As can be seen, a modular training of this kind requires a great degree of self-awareness on the part of the director to recognize areas of need and act on them. It also pre-supposes an accessible network of courses and attachments designed to supply the necessary modules, for instance a one-year acting course that a director can drop into.

Above all, it needs a well co-ordinated organizational structure to put directors in touch with the opportunities and to help them find the necessary funding. Under the present conditions it is a formidable and expensive task for anyone to plug the gaps in their training. Little wonder that few directors ever manage to do it.

d. Making it Happen

Clearly, the funding question is vital. Many more bursaries will need to be made available, and they must be flexible enough to cover a wide range of training situations and time scales. Also, the profession itself will have to be more prepared to open its doors to directors, accommodating all kinds of attachments and periods of observation.

It should be emphasized here that the film and television industry has long maintained a serious responsibility for training by providing both opportunities to observe and the funding for formal training. By contrast, the commercial theatre sector does not take any significant responsibility for training. As training is a form of investment, it is in the theatre's interest to revise its attitude.

Similarly, the higher education sector needs to look more seriously at the notion of mature and non-standard entry; that is, without the conventional academic qualifications. As directors will not all be young, and some will have had previous professional experience in related areas, post-experience will have to replace postgraduate status as a condition for entry. The Open University could be a useful model here.

IX

Indeed, the whole attitude of the 'bottleneck' situation (described in Chapter III) will have to be revised so that older directors have as equal an opportunity to train as young ones. This allows, of course, that prodigies will always be evident, but they will be the exception rather than a model to emulate.

Funding structures and grants will also have to be reorganized to recognize a training scheme that will take place in more than one institution - and one of those will be a professional theatre. Thus, a graduate going on to train in a drama school, or to take up an attachment as part of the training, should qualify for a mandatory grant just as a postgraduate student does.

3. Evaluation

The next stage is that the existing training must be evaluated in more detail than has been possible on this Enquiry. This is one reason why an independent co-ordinating body is vital, because it could carry out that assessment, overseeing the training and examining where the vocational meets the academic.

A training council therefore needs to be called together, comprising representatives of interested organizations such as Equity, The Directors Guild, ACTT and SCUDD. Also, any other organization that feels it is taking care of certain modules should be able to make a claim to be on this council.

4. Conclusion

The Enquiry has discussed these issues at length and is of the opinion that, in the short term, the realistic option is the modular approach. All efforts should be made to set up the mechanism that will enable this to operate as soon as possible.

At the same time, properly-funded three-year professional courses should be seen as real targets, even though it is realized that these may take a long while to set up. Therefore, it is important that the goal is kept within sight: the pressure to make it happen should begin now. Once in place, three-year courses and the modular network should complement each other to offer a training that will be flexible enough to respond to the diverse needs of British theatre, and thorough enough to launch a new wave of directors who will be as well-trained as any in the world. The components and the talent are already here: it is now a matter of using them.

Chapter X

Summary of Recommendations

CONCERNING THOSE WITH THE OVERVIEW

1 (a) We urge the Arts Council of Great Britain and the Calouste Gulbenkian Foundation to instigate the formation of a training council. They should invite representatives of interested organizations, including SCUDD, Equity, ACTT, The Directors Guild, ITI and ITC.

1 (b) This independent body, which might be called the Directors Training Council, should be set up to press for many of the recommendations that follow and to find ways in which the solutions outlined in Chapter IX might be implemented.

1 (c) Part of its remit should be to monitor training courses in live and recorded drama, both professional and within academic institutions. It would award accreditation to courses of sufficiently high standard.

1 (d) This body would also collate information on training opportunities and co-ordinate advanced study and research opportunities. It would also need the resources to monitor attachment schemes and to act as arbitrator, being prepared to intervene in the event of any conflict on the trainee or management's behalf.

2 The national theatres and opera companies need to examine their provisions for training in order to play their part in ensuring that there is a new generation of adequately trained directors.

3 Discussions between regional and touring theatres and their funding bodies should be set up to determine adequate policies on training, the priorities that they deserve, and how these might be achieved.

4 The Directors Guild, ITC and TMA should set up discussions with appropriate non-mainstream theatres - eg mime theatre, children's theatre, performance art, non-European theatre companies - to determine ways in which they might take a more active role in the training of directors. This might take the form of organizing short courses and workshops for directors, focusing on the company's area of expertise.

5 (a) Bodies such as TMA and SWET should be asked to consider ways in which West End and commercial productions could help to finance the training of directors. The example of the film and television industry could be followed: at present it provides almost half of the National Film and Television School's £3.4 million budget.

5 (b) TMA and SWET should be asked to set up a system whereby commercial and subsidized theatres could give passes to bona fide student directors so that they are encouraged to see as much theatre as possible.

6 Once the training of directors has been reformed, local authority grants for students taking part in these courses should be mandatory. This endorses the recommendation on drama schools made in the Cork Report, *Theatre is for All*.

7 The Government should ensure through the Independent Television Commission that broadcasting makes adequate provision for the training of directors for the film and television industries. The Enquiry has made a separate submission on this issue.

8 Cross-media links should be strengthened to facilitate theatre directors learning about film and television and vice versa.

9 The different cultural dimensions in Britain, which are reflected in non-English speaking theatres and non-western theatre techniques, should be acknowledged and provided for in any director training scheme so that minority-language groups and those wishing to explore non-European cultural traditions of theatre are in no way disadvantaged.

CONCERNING THE PROVIDERS OF TRAINING

Specific Needs

10 Those considering a director training course should ensure that the following points are included:

i) Learning how to work with actors and understanding the actor's processes should be the primary focus of any course on directing.

ii) Experienced actors should be employed as teachers as well as performers in director training courses across all media.

iii) There should be an examination of how the trainers themselves acquire their skills.

iv) There should be adequate opportunities for professional updating by academic staff.

v) Any system of director training, whether in a university, polytechnic, college or a drama school, should build effective links with the profession taking particular account of local theatre companies and professional facilities.

vi) Similarly, professional theatres should show a willingness to make useful contact with director training courses in their area, and they should be prepared to play a part in that training.

vii) Director training courses should include adequate guidance on the special skills needed for working with children and young people, in performances and workshops.

X

11 The provision for short courses in specific areas should be increased so that working directors can begin to fill gaps in their professional experience (eg technical skills such as lighting and design; or the use of improvisation, dance or mime).

12 Writers' organizations, such as the Writers' Guild and the Theatre Writers' Union, should approach the proposed Directors Training Council to discuss how work with writers could best be developed

i) on director training courses for theatre,

ii) on director training courses for film and television.

13(a) The managerial role of the director should be considered an integral part of director training.

13(b) Appropriate ways should be found for teaching group dynamics and people management.

13(c) Training opportunities outside the arts should be investigated, eg what the commercial sector can offer in management skills.

CONCERNING THE PROVIDERS OF BURSARIES, ATTACHMENT AND OBSERVER SCHEMES

14(a) A list should be completed and regularly updated of artistic directors in different types of theatre who are willing to host trainees on attachment. This would enable trainee schemes and candidates to streamline their contacts.

14(b) A list should be completed and regularly updated of directors in all media who are willing to accept observers on their productions.

14(c) Attachment and bursary schemes should make a careful survey of the strengths and weaknesses of eligible receiving theatres. Discussions should be set up in advance with the artistic directors of these theatres to determine their commitment to the training scheme and to assess their ability to provide a suitable training programme.

14(d) A working party of artistic directors should be set up to determine ways in which attachments might be made more efficient and fulfilling, both for the receiving theatre and the trainee. Thought should also be given to the appropriate length of time for an attachment, and at what point, if at all, the trainee could be given a production to direct.

14(e) Attachment schemes should make adequately-funded provisions for the monitoring of the attachments that have been set up, and also for a better system of collecting information on the success or otherwise of particular attachments.

14(f) The selection procedure for attachment schemes and bursaries needs to be re-examined and revised according to the principles of equal opportunity with no specific age limit which would include and encourage prospective directors who have had previous training and/or other relevant professional experience.

CONCERNING THE PROVIDERS OF FILM AND TELEVISION TRAINING

15 Film and television courses should make greater provision for

i) the understanding of the acting process and working with actors,

ii) the process of developing a script in collaboration with a writer,

iii) adequate exposure within the curriculum of students to a wide range of film and television culture.

16 Trainee television directors should spend an appropriate period of time working in the various departments that are involved in studio production in order to gain a clearer understanding of the resources and facilities available to them.

X

APPENDIX A

BRITISH ACTORS' EQUITY SUBMISSION

Introduction

We do not intend to take an inordinate proportion of this paper arguing the need for a change from the status quo in the training of directors since the very existence of the Gulbenkian Enquiry presupposes that the arguments for change made over the last few years by Equity (and many other bodies and individuals) have already had their effect.

Suffice it to say that the present ad hoc system is inadequate and uneconomic. Also, its in-built bias towards prospective directors whose only experience is that of university drama means that many young directors go into the profession totally unable to deal with the needs of the professional actor. Despite a small minority of talented exceptions, many young directors only manage to 'get away' with productions because they have been 'saved' by the abilities of their highly trained and experienced actors and production team. The present (much vocalised and publicised) distrust of directors by many actors is largely a result of the present 'system' of ad hoc training.

To put this paper into context, it should perhaps be pointed out that - although it emanates from British Actors' Equity - it has been prepared by a committee of experienced professional directors whose experiences of the status quo have made them all too aware of the inadequacy of their own training and who therefore wish to ensure a better future for future generations of directors.

The rest of this paper therefore sets out to suggest the basis for an effective structure for the training of directors in Britain.

Basic Organisation of the Course

The course we propose would be a national three-year one and it would be open to selected apprentice directors throughout Britain. Stages One and Two of the course (although not Stage Three) would also be open to foreign nationals. This would both help the financing of such a course by bringing in outside finance and also help the British apprentices by giving them a broader context of experience from fellow apprentices on which to draw.

There would be no maximum age limit for entrance since the course would be a postgraduate one looking for apprentices who already have previous experience on which to build. One of the problems of the present 'young' directors training schemes is that they heavily discriminate against women (who may have taken time out to bring up children and who therefore already possess valuable knowledge about 'people' management) and experienced actors who have something to contribute through a change of career.

Since there are - by the nature of things - far fewer openings for new directors than for new actors and since it is desirable for the number of entrants each year to be in proportion to the potential job opportunities, we envisage a single national course rather than a variety of separate courses throughout Britain. However, the danger of a single national course is that it could aspire to turn out a unified 'standard' type of director rather than to develop and train the potential talent of individuals.

To guard against this danger, the course should not take place in one (probably London-based) institution. Instead, the different stages of the course should be allocated in turn to different drama schools, theatres and (for elements of Stage One) university drama departments throughout the country who would put up bids for the opportunity of running a particular module of the course. We view it as particularly important that university drama departments and other purely academic institutions such as polytechnics should only be able to bid for parts of Stage One of the course since it is *essential* that the rest of the course be purely practical and not academic.

In this way, the apprentice director would move round Britain during the course and gain a wide variety of experience of the different types of work being done in the profession. Such a 'mobile' course might be unsettling for young people who need a settled environment but the experienced apprentices who are desirable for this course would be already used to the transitory life that is part and parcel of the profession.

The Panel and The Secretariat

Such a 'modular' course at different institutions would require an organizational structure which is separate from the institutions at which the 'modules' take place. We envisage that this structure would consist of a small administrative secretariat which would be responsible to a policy panel. The secretariat would be responsible for organizing the paperwork and finance of the course and generally for servicing and putting into effect the decisions of the policy panel. The secretariat would be based in an office which was geographically central to Britain and convenient for access by road and rail.

The policy panel would consist of a majority of experienced professional directors - along with a sprinkling of educationalists and related professionals there to add diversity. It would meet for an intensive week once a year to plan the course for the following year and thereafter on a regular basis throughout each year in order to review progress and interview and select potential apprentices. In order to ensure a constant flux of new ideas on the panel and to guard against any rigid formula of training, a quarter of the panel would be replaced each year by new members appointed by the Department of Education (or whichever body was ultimately responsible for the course).

The idea of the panel consisting largely of working directors is intrinsic to the conception of the course - following from the medieval practice of craftsmen passing on their knowledge to apprentices. Each director on the panel would (in the second of their four years on the panel) take on a number of the new apprentice directors and act as their 'preceptor' (or mentor). Each apprentice would therefore have a preceptor throughout the three years of the course whom the apprentice would regularly visit to discuss progress. Each preceptor would at all times make their work processes open to observation by those of their apprentices who were visiting them.

In order to ensure a series of checks and balances within the system, there should be provision for external examiners who would help to verify the worthiness of the work of the apprentices and see that justice is done to them. Any apprentices having difficulty in relating to their preceptor could turn to the external examiner for advice. The external examiners could also help resolve tensions when they are sure that the problem in hand is that an element in the course is wrong for the apprentice rather than the apprentice wrong for the course.

Essential Previous Experience for Apprentices

Since a theatre director is (in essence) a leader who originates interpretive ideas in regard to a production and co-ordinates the separate elements of the production into a unified whole, the three basic areas of experience necessary to the job are as follows:

(a) The acting process: this can only be appreciated by having direct personal professional experience of acting. It does not mean that the would-be director need have been a good actor but that they have been in the position of understanding the process - no matter how inadequate their performance.

(b) Technical, administrative and managerial experience: stage management, electrics, lighting design, sound, costume, design, budgets, basic administrative practices and the management of people and their problems (rather than just the management of resources). A few years ago, it was not necessary for theatre directors to know much about budgets and administration unless they were actually running a building or a company. In the present British theatre set-up, it is essential for a director to be well versed in these areas.

(c) The academic background: a knowledge of theatre and society throughout the ages, a wide repertoire of classical and contemporary drama, art styles and design methods, music, text analysis, etc.

It is both usual and necessary for any apprentice director to possess a fairly comprehensive background in one of these areas. Unfortunately, it is very much the exception rather than the rule for a student director to have experience in more than one area.

The Three Stage Course

The training would consist of three stages. It is probable that (for ease of administration) each stage would take one year - although this could be more flexible if it was desirable.

Stage One

In this initial stage, the apprentice directors study (and practise) the areas in which their knowledge and experience is deficient. Therefore, the actor studies the academic, stage management, administrative and managerial background; the technically and managerially experienced apprentice studies acting and the academic background; the university graduate studies acting, stage management, administration and management. As indicated above, the apprentices are split up and go to whatever courses in the country have been arranged as appropriate by the panel.

Stage Two

The apprentice directors can now be assumed to have a common general knowledge in all the necessary background areas - even if their experience still differs in degrees as individuals. They are now brought together to work in one institution (which could be changed each year). The purpose of this core stage of the course is for the apprentices to tackle the central problem of exploring the three-way relationship between the director, the actor and the text.

To begin with, the apprentices would take turns to direct their fellow apprentices in workshops of scenes selected by supervising tutors. They would also throughout the year take time out to observe the rehearsals of a variety of professional directors and work with tutors on the practical preparation/analysis of the texts which they are workshopping.

In the second half of the year, the course would employ a small core of experienced professional actors on a six-month contract to play the leading roles in the workshop scenes and full-scale plays directed by the apprentices. (The minor roles would be taken by the other apprentices.) Now the apprentices would direct plays and scenes of their own choosing and cast them (from the actors and other apprentices) in consultation with the tutors. Each apprentice would direct one full length production and two scenes. The eventual performances of the plays and programmes of scenes would be open to an invited audience of tutors, preceptors, prospective employers, fellow apprentices from other stages of the course and anybody else thought appropriate.

These performances would be without benefit of scenery, costume or lighting. This would be partly for reasons of economics and to avoid employing any technical back-up. However, it would also encourage the concentration of this part of the course on the central relationship between director, actor and text. However, the apprentices would work with their tutors (as well as designers, lighting designers, etc brought in as guest lecturers) to explore the staging possibilities of the plays and scenes on which they are working.

One other aspect that it would be desirable for the apprentice to explore during this stage of the course would be the differing disciplines involved in direction in theatre, television and film. With the increasing afterlife of stage production on video in the current media scene and the proliferation of directors who work in more than one medium, it would be useful for the apprentices to study doing scenes in all three media. Apprentices who discover a particular aptitude and interest in film and/or television could then go on to train further in these media rather than progressing to Stage Three of the course.

Stage Three

These apprentice directors who had successfully completed the first two stages of the course and were considered suitable by the panel would then be seconded to a professional theatre and/or theatre company by arrangement with Artistic Directors who had already seen their work in Stage Two. (These theatres could be reps, fringe or touring companies but should not be large institutions like the Royal Shakespeare Company or the Royal National Theatre where the apprentice would tend to get lost in the 'machinery'. Also, no theatre or company should have more than one apprentice assigned to it at any one time.)

During this stage of the course, the apprentice would participate in succession in various departments of the theatre in an observer or (whenever possible) practising assistant position and then go on to work with the head of each department in a theoretical exercise about the previous production. For example (assuming a season whose first three productions were *Hamlet*, *Three Sisters* and a pantomime), the apprentice might work as assistant electrician on *Hamlet* and then work in the box office and observe in the admin office on *Three Sisters*. During *Three Sisters* rehearsals the apprentice would also work on an exercise with the resident lighting designer about how the apprentice might have lit *Hamlet*. During the pantomime rehearsals, the apprentice would work with the administrator on budgeting a projected season.

This would go on to develop throughout the season in succession to include design, stage management, publicity, being an assistant director, casting and dealing with agents, working with authors as a script editor on new plays, reading and assessing new plays and (particularly important) acting. We consider it vital that the apprentices have the experience of acting professionally in two productions during the year (no matter how minor the role) so that they experience the differing demands and rhythms of rehearsal and repeated performance from an actor's point of view. However, in order to prevent the apprentices being exploited as cheap 'cast fillers', they should not be allowed to appear in more than two productions and any apprentice who has previously acted professionally should *not* be allowed to act during Stage Three.

As the year progresses, the apprentice would increasingly work alongside the artistic director and accompany them to board meetings, meetings with funders and meetings with authors, etc. An important element would be the gaining of experience in dealing with outside bodies (such as the Arts Council, RAAs and sponsors) and the mechanics of preparing grant applications. Towards the end of the year, the apprentice would be guaranteed at least one full-scale production to direct.

Further Progress

The progress of each of the apprentices at the end of Stage Three would then be assessed by the panel in co-operation with the Artistic Directors with whom each apprentice has worked. Those apprentices who were considered to have satisfactorily completed the course would be given a certificate. In order to ease their entry into the profession they would be able to approach the theatre in which they have been working (or any other theatre) and offer themselves as a resident director for a year at the cost to the theatre of half the minimum salary (the other half would be paid for as a bursary by the course). Any theatre which took up this offer would have to guarantee the director (no longer considered an apprentice) at least two productions to direct.

Funding

It is not our intention to go into detail about the financing of such a course since these matters are largely outside our areas of experience. However, we would envisage that the first two stages of the course (which we have tried to set out in cost-effective terms) would require central funding. Stage Three and the further progress bursaries would gradually replace the Arts Council and television sponsored bursaries and we therefore consider that they should be paid for by a fund set up by the Arts Council, and the theatre and television industries.

Conclusion

The course would develop a system for fully and adequately training directors to the standards that has long produced such fine standards of acting in this country. The continually evolving environments and staffing of the course should avoid any danger of a regimented 'standard' apprentice and the aim should be to encourage and develop the individual ideas and enthusiasms of each apprentice in a responsible context.

Although we envisage that the majority of new directors would go through this course, it is important to point out that it would not prevent people becoming directors by other means by means of their exceptional talent. In particular, fringe theatre would continue to throw up interesting new directors whose ideas and abilities would continually challenge such a course to reassess its standards.

However, the result of such a course would be a comprehensive and systematic apprenticeship which - given the crucial importance of the role of the director in a production - would have immediate and lasting benefit to the overall standard of British theatre.

APPENDIX B

NAMES OF CONTRIBUTORS TO THE ENQUIRY

Individual Written Evidence

Eric Allan	Director, Television & Radio
Michael Baker	Director of Drama, Welsh Arts Council
Clive Barker	Director
James Barlow	Director
Monika Barnes	Training Manager, Thames Television
Christopher Barry	Television Director
James Barton	Director, Jactito Puppets
Christopher Baugh	Designer
Alistair Black	General Adviser (Drama) Hampshire County Council
Keith Boak	Director
Chris Bond	ex-Director, Half Moon Theatre
Edward Bond	Playwright
John Bowen	Playwright
Mark Brickman	Director, Actors Touring Company
Peter Brook	Director, Centre International de Créations Théâtrales
Kate Brown	Director, Opera
Michael Bryant	Actor
Nigel Bryant	Director, Orchard Theatre
Howard Burell	Director, Opera East
Katie Campbell	Playwright
Roy Campbell-Moore	Director, Diversions Dance Company
James Cairncross	Actor
Penny Casdagli	Director, Neti-Neti Theatre Company
Deborah Chadbourn	Administrator, Arts Admin
Ned Chaillet	Script Editor, Plays, BBC Radio 3
Sally Cook	Mime
Peter Copley	Actor
David Cregan	Playwright
Ivan Cutting	Director, East Angles Theatre Company
Elinor Day	Director
Anne Dennis	Actor, director, drama teacher
Anthea Dobry	Director
Anne Downie	Actor, playwright
Simon Dunmore	Director
Gwyn Lloyd Evans	Director, Television
John Fox	Artistic Director, Welfare State International
Roger Gregory	Script Editor, BBC Midlands
Robert Hamlin	Artistic Director, Belgrade Theatre, Coventry
Philip Harland	Director, Film & Video
Wally Hazlehurst	Television Lighting Designer
Jonathan Holloway	Director, Red Shift Theatre Company
Anthony Hopkins	Actor
Sir Michael Hordern	Actor

178

Vicky Ireland	Director, Polka Children's Theatre
Glenda Jackson	Actor
Alby James	Artistic Director, Temba
Martin Jameson	Artistic Director, Nottingham Playhouse
Pat Keysell	Mime
Don Kinch	Artistic Director, African Peoples Theatre
Maggie Kinloch	Director
Leonard Lewis	Director, Television
Peter Lichtenfels	Artistic Director, Haymarket Theatre, Leicester
Patrick Masefield	Regional Arts Consultant
Roddy Maude-Roxby	Director
Rick Mellis	Director, Television
Stella Moray	Actor
Jane Morgan	Stagemanager
John Mowat	Mime
Kathleen McCreery	Director
Andrew McKinnon	Artistic Director, Tyne Theatre Company
Dereck Nicholls	Artistic Director, The Birmingham Repertory Theatre
Sue Nott	Producer, Central Television
Jamie Nuttgens	Director
Jon Oram	Artistic Director, Colway Theatre Trust
Robert Ornbo	Director
Christopher Oxford	Director
Ronan Paterson	Artistic Director, Northumberland Theatre Company
Jean Perkins	Actor
Michael Poeynor	Director
John Pope	Director, The Shadow Syndicate
Bill Pryde	Artistic Director, Cambridge Theatre Company
Roland Rees	ex-Artistic Director, Foco Novo Theatre Company
Max Roberts	Director, Live Theatre Company Ltd
Robert Robertson	Director, Dundee Repertory Theatre
Laurance Sach	Director, Durham Theatre Company
Gregory Smith	Designer
Les Smith	Playwright
Alan Strachan	Artistic Director, Greenwich Theatre
Kenneth Alan Taylor	Artistic Director, Nottingham Playhouse
Robert Tomlinson	Director, Television, Western Eye
Clare Venables	Artistic Director, Crucible Theatre
Glen Walford	Artistic Director, Everyman Theatre
Chris Wallis	Director, Unicorn Theatre
Sam Walters	Director, Orange Tree Theatre
Juliet Watkinson	Designer, Chester Gateway Theatre
Charles Way	Playwright
Nina Weaver	TV Vision Mixer

Individual Oral Evidence

Tim Albery	Director
Bill Alexander	Director
Jack Andrews	Administrator, RTYDS
Annabel Arden	Director, Théâtre de Complicité
Dame Peggy Ashcroft	Actor
Sir Richard Attenborough	Director
Julia Bardsley	Director
Jean Benedetti	Director
Cicely Berry	Director of Voice, Royal Shakespeare Company
David Bintley	Choreographer
John Burgess	Associate Director, Royal National Theatre Studio
Sue Charman	Artistic Director, Solent Peoples Theatre
Brian Cox	Actor
Dame Judi Dench	Actor
Declan Donnellan	Artistic Director, Cheek by Jowl
Richard Eyre	Artistic Director, Royal National Theatre
Peter Gill	Director, Royal National Theatre Studio
Jack Gold	Director
Simon McBurney	Director, Théâtre de Complicité
Donald McIntyre	Opera singer
Sir Peter Hall	Director
Terry Hands	Artistic Director, Royal Shakespeare Company
Loretta Howells	Training Officer, Arts Council of Great Britain
Jonathan Miller	Artistic Director, Old Vic Theatre
Christopher Morahan	Director
Oliver Neville	Principal, Royal Academy of Dramatic Art
Trevor Nunn	Director
Jonathan Pope	Drama Officer, Arts Council of Great Britain
David Puttnam	Film Producer
Virginia Snyders	Head of Drama, Guildhall School of Music and Drama
Max Stafford-Clark	Artistic Director, Royal Court Theatre
Donald Sumpter	Actor
Stephen Unwin	Director
Deborah Warner	Director
Arnold Wesker	Playwright
Noel Witts	Head of Drama, Leicester Polytechnic

Individual Evidence through the Questionnaire to Directors

William Aaron
Keith Ackrill
B Adams
Gary Adams
Jad Adams
Doug Aitken
Dorothea Alexander
Anthony Allen
Julian Amyes
Alan Anderson
Lindsay Anderson
Keith Andrews
Gus Angus
Tim Appelbee
Sallie Aprahamian
Catharine Arakelian
Annabel Arden
Richard Argent
Moira Armstrong
Harvey Ashby
Philip Ashby
Michael Attenborough
Alan Ayckbourn

Caroline Baker
Celia Bannerman
Dominic Barber
Clive Barker
Jonathan Barker
Nicholas Barker
James Barlow
Peter Barlow
Christopher Barry
Chris Barton
John Barton
Michael Bath
Roy Battersby
Stephen Bayly
Randal Beattie
Lutz Becker
Michael Becker
Piers Bedford
Terry Bedford

George Bekes
Alec Bell
Charles Bell
Ivor Benjamin
Stuart Bennett
Bogdan Berciu
Frances Berrigan
Jim Berrow
Susanna Best

James Cellan-Jones
Ned Chaillet
Hazel Chandler
Mark Chapman
Peter Charlton
Piers Chater-Robinson
Les Chatfield
Penny Cherns
Roger Cheveley
Greg Childs
John Chilvers
Tony Church
Peter Claridge
Caryne Clark
Michael Clarke
Barry Clayton
Roger Clissold
Chris Clough
Teresa Collard
Richard Collin
P H Coltman
Shane Connaughton
Adrian Cooper
Peter Cooper
Paul Cordsen
Anthony Cornish
Tom Cotter
Vivienne Cottrel
Richard Cottrell
Frank Cox
Michael Coyle
Vivienne Cozens
Bob Cramp

Peter Cregeen
Mike Crisp
Gilles Croft
John Crome
David Crosse
David Crossman
Brian Croucher
Roger Crougher
Mike Crowson
David Crozier
Bernard Cullen
Fiona Cumming
Simon Curtis
Ivan Cutting

Michael Darlow
William Dashwood
David Datta
John David
John Davies
Mike Davies
Desmond Davis
Tamasin Day Lewis
James Dearden
Glyn Dearman
Christopher De Sovea
Peter Dews
Peter Diamond
Julia Dickinson
William Dickinson
Fisher Dilke
Nancy Diuguid
Clive Donner
Mike Dormer
Mark Dornford-May
Wallace Douglas
Valerie Doulton
Taylor Downing
Rex Doyle
Peter Duffewl
Han Duijvendak
Christopher Dunham
Simon Dunmore

Alan Dunnett
Richard Duployen
Terry Dyddgen-Jones
Wendy Dyer

Bob Eaton
Michael Eaton
Christine Eccles
Barry Edwards
Michael Elwyn
George Eugeniou
David Evans
Caroline Eves
Ronald Eyre

Simon Fallon
Brian Farnham
Dianne Farris
James Fawcett
Richard Fawkes
Eleanor Fazan
Rachel Feldberg
Malcolm Feuerstein
Vanessa Fielding
Mike Figgis
Nigel Finch
Nicholas Fine
Michael Finlason
Chris Fisher
Tony Fisher
Robert Fleming
Mike Florence
Maggie Ford
Peter Ford
David Forder
John Fox
Ron Francis
William Franklyn
Sally Freeman
Brian Freeston
Martyn Friend
Terence Frisby

Chris Gage
David Gaines
Lyril Gates

Jon Gaunt
Marilyn Gaunt
David Giles
Peter Gill
Kieran Gillespie
Robert Gillespie
Andrew Gillman
David Gilmore
David Gladwell
Susan Glanville
John Glenister
John Godber
Colin Godman
Keith Godman
Robert Golden
Hugh Goldie
Sally Goldsworthy
Derrick Goodwin
Nigel Gordon
John Gorrie
Richard Gough
Sebastian Graham-
    Jones
D R Graham-Young
Charles Gregson
Andrew Grieve
Ronald Guariento
Mollie Guilfoyle

Richard Hackett
John Hall
Maggie Hall
Tony Halton
Mira Hamermesh
Gloria Hamilton
Robert Hamlin
Sheila Hancock
Richard Handford
Sarah Harding
Terry Harding
Charles Harris
Sebastian Harris
Vivien Harris
Gerry Harrison
Wilfred Harrison
David Hart

Francis Harvey
Giles Havergal
Tom Hawkes
Chris Hayes
Carloe Hayman
Philip Hedley
David Hedley-
    Williams
Leona Heimfeld
Sarah Hellings
Norman Castle
    Hemsley
John Henderson
John Heyer
Karl Hibbert
Andrew Higgs
Ken Hill
Andrew Hilton
David Hodgson
Christopher Hodson
Dean Hollingsworth
Jonathan Holloway
Christopher Honer
Laurence Honeyford
Martin Hooghton
Ken Howard
William Howe
Jane Howell
Richard Howson
Michael Hucks
Brian Hulls
Chris Hunt
Hugh Hunt
Simon Hutchens
Barri Hutchin
Lesley Hutchison
David Hutt
Marilyn Hyndman

Terence Iland
Faith Isiakpere
Mehmet Izbudak

Jane Jackson
Paul Jackson
Alby James

Pedr James
M Japp
Eric Jarvis
Jason Jay
Ann Jellicoe
Marie Jenkin
Brian Jenkinson
A Jones
David Jones
Desmond Jones
Ellis Jones
Huw Jones
Andy Jordan
Wilfred Judd
Ian Judge

Maurice Kanareck
Marek Kanievska
Russ Kapel
Jerzy Kaszwbowski
Helena Kauf-Housen
John Keefe
Jude Kelly
Nicholas Kelsey
Richard Kempton
Roy Kendall
Rosalind King
T Kingdon
Deborah Kingsland
J Peter Kinkead
Alex Kirby
Ian Knox
Sam Kogan
Anthony Kovacs
Barry Kyle

Jeremy Lack
John Ladle
Robert Lamrock
Jill Lamede
Harry Landis
Btugid Larmour
Leslie Lawton
Susan Learwood
Sue Lefton
Mike Leigh

Barry Letts
Peter Levelle
Leonard Lewis
Anita Lewton
Jonathan Lichtensten
Julia Limer
Matthew Lloyd
Mike Lloyd
Martin Locke
R Lomas
Mary Longford
Alan Lovell
Alan Lowery
Martin Lucas
Mike Lucas
Colin Luke
Roger Lunn
Maureen Lunt
John Lynch
Jonathan Lynn
Gillian Lynne

Ian McArthur
Desmond McCarthy
John McColgan
Jeremy McCracken
James MacDonald
Stephen MacDonald
Linda McDougall
Ian McKeand
Juliet McKoen
Ian McMillan
Lynne McVernon
Lorne Magory
John Mair
Andrew Manley
Stacy Markin
Jeremy Marre
Robin Marriott
Robert Marshall
David Martin
Jonathan Martin
Bill Mason
Bim Mason
Libby Mason
William Mather

Patrick Maunsell
A Maxwell-Hyslop
Royston Mayoh
Nancy Meckler
Richard Mervyn
Steve Mesure
John Metcalfe
Roger Michell
Robin Midgley
Mari Miller
Scott Miller
Leslie Mills
J Edward Milner
Ian Milton
Bill Miskelly
A Mitchell
Katie Mitchell
David Mitton
Eric Mival
Paul Moreus
Andrew Morgan
Brian Morgan
Di Morgan
Natasha Morgan
Bernard Morris
Michael Morris
Don Morrison
Paul Morrison
Moushegh Moughalian
Gerard Mulgrew
Ian Mullins
Stuart Mungall
David Munro
Braham Murray
Jonathan Myerson

John Nash
Adrin Neatrour
Roy Nevitt

Jim O'Brien
P O'Shea
Philip Osment
Christopher Oxford
Olusola Oyeleye

Tony Palmer
Brian Parker
Ann Parnell McGarry
Sue Parrish
Julia Pascal
Ronan Paterson
Willie Patterson
Heather Peace
Ewan Pearson
Patricia Pearson
David Peason
Birte Pederson
Mark Petersen
Chris Pettit
Helen Petts
David Phethean
Caroline Pick
G David Pick
Tim Piers
Maggie Pinhorn
Mark Piper
Nicholas Pitt
John Pluck
Nicholas Pole
Johanna Pool
Angela Pope
Bunmi Popoola
Denis Postle
Gerry Poulson
Michael Poyner
Tony Price
Nicholas Prosser
David Proudfood
John Prowse
Philip Prowse
Bill Pryde
Peter Pullon

A J Quinn
Michael Quinn

Michael Radford
Alvin Rakoff
Alasdair Ramsay
Harry Rankin
Caroline Raphael

Alan Ravenscroft
Christopher Rawlence
Ben Rea
Roland Rees
Alastair Reid
Alec Reid
Nicholas Renton
Adrian Reynolds
Bob Ricards
Beryl Richards
Frances Rifkin
Stephen Ripley
Alwyn Roberts
Pennant Roberts
G Robertson
K Angus Robertson
Sid Robertson
Toby Robertson
Anton Rodgers
Alan Rodman
Michael Rolfe
Colin Rose
Alan Ross
Howard Ross
Adrian Rowbothan
Chris Rowbury
Peter Rowe
Kenneth Rowles
Paul Roylance
Sandra Rudkin
Paddy Russell
Renny Rye

Laurence Sach
Chattie Salaman
Diane Samuels
Patrick Sandford
Peter Sasdy
Mark Saunders
John Schlesinger
Tony Scull
Francis Sealey
Paul Seed
Sayed Shah
D Cameron Shaw
Margaret Sheehy

Brian Shelton
Sue Shephard
John Sheppard
Ceri Sherlock
Debbie Shewell
Mike Shoring
Robert Sian
Pat Silburn
Anthony Simmons
Brian Simmons
Brenda Simpson
Michael Simpson
Leon Sinden
Gurdial Sira
Neil Sissons
Alison Skilbeck
Julian Sluggett
Anthony Smith
Frank Smith
Kevin Smith
Martin Smith
Roger Smith
Wendy Smith
Sharon Smullen
Brian Spencer
John Spencer
Max Stafford-Clark
Tom Steel
Helena Stevens
John Stokes
Penny Stokes
Karen Stone
Alan Strachan
Pam Strachan
Toni Strasburg
David Street
Ann Stutfield
Ian Stuttard
David Sulkin
Shelley Sulton
Jeremy Sutcliffe
Roger Swaine
Christopher Swann
Geoffrey Sykes
Richard Syns

David Taylor
Kenneth Taylor
Malcolm Taylor
Richard Taylor
Jeff Teare
David Thacker
Anthony Thomas
Colen Thomas
Ed Thomason
David Thomasson
Jenny Thompson
Paul Thompson
Caroline Tisdall
Ron Trickett
David Tucker
Anthony Tuckey
David Tudor
David Turnbull
Patrick Turley
P Turner
Benjamin Twist
John Tydeman
Robert Tyrrell

Stuart Urban

Christa Van Raalte
Jay Vaughan
Jatinder Verma
Clare Verook
Andrew Visnevski

Peter Walker
Philippa Walker
Rob Walker
Clare Walters
Sam Walters
Barry Warden
Deborah Warner
Adrian Warren
Keith Washington
Doc Watson
Mark Watters
Geofrey Weaver
Sue Weeks
Victoria Wegg-Posser
Don Weinstein
Diane West
Hilary Westlake

John Whiston
Leonard White
Faynia Williams
Margaret Williams
Terence Williams
Jackie Willows
Alan Wilson
Ronald Wilson
Jane Winter
Herbert Wise
Carol Wiseman
Debbie Wolfe
Kathryn Wolfe
Peter Wollen
Stuart Wood
Mark Woolgar
John Wright
Ian Wyatt
Maureen Wynne
Peter Wynne-Willson

Michele Young

Rick Zoltowski

Written Evidence from Organizations

Anglia Television Limited
British Actors' Equity Association
Central Independent Television plc
Directors Guild of Great Britain
Howard Steel Foundation
Independent Television Association
Independent Theatre Council
John Fernald Award
Scottish Television plc
Standing Committee of University Drama Departments
Thames Television plc
Writers' Guild of Great Britain
Yorkshire Television

Regional Meetings

LONDON - 16TH JULY 1988:

Trevor Stuart	Actor
Paul Jacobs	Actor
David Swift	Actor
Joanna Maude	Actor
Sarah-Jane McKechnie	Actor
Karen Gledhill	Actor
Will Perry	Drama Student
Claire Mason	Stagemanager
Belinda Ackerman	Designer
David Toguri	Choreographer
Stuart Hopps	Choreographer
Imogen Claire	Choreographer
Charles Lewsen	Actor, playwright, teacher
Sarah Pia Anderson	Director
Nancy Meckler	Artistic Director, Shared Experience
Les Blair	Director, Film
Leonard White	Director
Claire Grove	Director, Derby Playhouse Studio
Alby James	Artistic Director, Temba
Darrol Blake	Director

BRISTOL - 23RD JULY 1988:

Jo Anderson	Playwright
Sheila Yeger	Playwright
Patrick Malahide	Actor
Iain Stuart-Ferguson	Choreographer
Marina Caldaroni	Assistant Director, Clywd
Roy Campbell-Moore	Director, Diversion Dance Company
Steve Shill	Director
Paul Unwin	Artistic Director, Bristol Old Vic
Martin White	Bristol University Drama Dept

LONDON - 25TH JULY 1988:

Paul Mead	Choreographer
Denni Sayers	Choreographer
Philip Fox	Actor
Tamsin Heatley	Actor
Peter Howell	Actor
Liz McKechnie	Actor
Alison Skilbeck	Actor
David Ayliff	Stagemanager
Rob King	TV Floor Manager
Alison Chitty	Designer

David Rose	Head of Drama, Channel-4
Ned Chaillet	Script Editor, BBC Radio Drama
Nicholas Barter	Director, ex Unicorn
Stuart Burge	Director
Philip Headley	Artistic Director, Theatre Royal Stratford East
Susan Hogg	Director, Radio
Michael Moxham	Director
Nicky Pallot	Artistic Director, The Bush Theatre
Debbie Shewell	Artistic Director, The Bush Theatre
David Thacker	Artistic Director, Young Vic,
Hilary Westlake	Artistic Director, Lumière & Son

LONDON (OPERA) - 26TH JULY 1988

Kate Brown	Producer, Scottish Opera
Claire Foden	Administrator, Opera 80
Wilfred Judd	Staff Producer, The Royal Opera House
Belinda Quirey	Choreographer
Jeremy Sutcliffe	Resident Producer,The Royal Opera House
David Taylor	Lighting designer

LEEDS - 30TH JULY 1988

Annie Castledine	Artistic Director, Derby Playhouse
Frances McNeil	Playwright
John Harrison	Artistic Director, Leeds Playhouse
Peter Lichtenfels	Artistic Director, Haymarket Theatre, Leicester
Kate Rowland	Associate Director, Playhouse, Liverpool

GLASGOW - 6TH AUGUST 1988

Alex McCrindle	Actor
John Christie	Actor
Alison Creswell	Assistant Stage Manager
Elizabeth Curruthers	Assistant Director, Perth
Morag Fullerton	Director, Borderline Theatre
Giles Havergal	Director, Glasgow Citizens
Flloyd Kennedy	Actor
Alan Lyddiad	Artistic Director, Tag Theatre
Kate McCall	Television floor manager
Sheelagh McCabe	Stage Manager
Joyce McMillan	Critic
Charles Nowosielki	Artistic Director, Theatre Alba
Stewart Laing	Designer
Sheridan Nicoll	Choreographer
Sheila Penson	Stage Manager
James Ross	Stage Manager
Cathy Strachan	Designer

MANCHESTER - 26TH SEPTEMBER 1988

Roy Barber	Actor
Mary Cunningham	Actor
Jim Linacre	Actor
Sandra Maitland	Actor
Simon Molloy	Actor
Kevin Newsham	Actor
Barbara Pearson	Actor
Alan Rothwell	Actor

CARDIFF - 15TH OCTOBER 1988

Ruth Garnault	Wales Actors Company
Richard Gough	Artistic Director, Cardiff Laboratory Theatre
Bethan Jones	Artistic Director, Dalier Sylw
Gruff Jones	Director
Graham Laker	Theatre Gwynedd
Deklan Leverton	Director, Paupers Carnival
Geoff Moore	Artistic Director, Moving Being
Charmian Saville	Clywd Outreach
Nigel Watson	Director, Theatre Taliesin

LONDON (WRITERS' GUILD) - 29TH SEPTEMBER 1988

Tony Craig	Playwright
Alan Drury	Playwright
David Edgar	Playwright
Pam Gems	Playwright
Anthony Minghella	Playwright
James Pettifer	Playwright
Nicholas Wright	Playwright
Stephen Wyatt	Playwright
Olwen Wymark	Playwright

Visits to Courses - 1988

Theatre

Bristol Old Vic Theatre School
British Theatre Association
University of Bristol
Dartington College
Drama Centre
The Drama Studio London
Glasgow University
Goldsmiths' College
Hull University
Leeds University
University of Kent at Canterbury
Middlesex Polytechnic - Trent Park
Middlesex Polytechnic - Ivy House
Royal Scottish Academy of Music and Drama

Film and Television

University of Bristol
London School of Printing
London International Film School
Royal College of Art
National Film and Television School

Other Schemes

BP Young Directors Festival
Regional Theatre Young Directors Scheme

Index